Sneak Attack

David Hatton

This is a work of fiction. All the characters and events portrayed in this book are either products of the author's imagination or are used fictitiously.

SNEAK ATTACK

Copyright © 2006 by David Hatton

ISBN: 978-0-6151-3719-3

Table of Contents

Snipe Hunt

It must have been in the fall of my ninth year when my older brother volunteered to take me on a snipe hunt. He explained that a snipe was a little furry animal whose pelt was very valuable in the fall of the year when its fur was newly grown, thick and luxurious. He proposed that if I would come and hold the sack that the snipes were to run into, I would get the biggest share of the profits. Ordinarily I would have been suspicious of any deal made to me by my bro on the grounds that it would be good for me. I had already been taught to be wary of anyone who expressed a fervid but false solicitude for the unfortunate over whom they sought mastery but our good friends and neighbors were there and they verified the facts as described by my brother.

They explained that the reason that I would get the biggest share was that it was very hard to sit still enough so the snipes wouldn't be scared away and I was about the most patient boy in the neighborhood. Besides it was a cool fall day and I might get cold but that too was the reason I would profit most. As we walked to the juniper covered hills a mile south of town, the area most likely to yield a good catch of snipes the boys all talked about what they were going to buy with their money.

We found the spot perfect to set the trap for the snipes, a dark shady spot in the fork of a tree with a well worn path through it obviously used by small animals. It looked like a rabbit path to me but they assured me that snipes were about the size of a big rabbit. That is why I could hold them so easily in the sack. I was to position myself on the down hill side of the tree with the gunny sack positioned in the fork of the tree where the snipes were sure to run. The rest of the gang was to walk in a big circle at designated speed so as to arrive in place at a designated time. Half the gang went west and half went east. Imagine if you will a circle out to the south of my hiding place ever tightening to frighten the snipes down the path and into the sack in my hiding place.

No sooner had they left, taking all their flattery and praise with them, suspicions once again assailed me. Just about two minutes of crouching in the cold dark hideaway convinced me that I had been suckered. Feeling somewhat stupid I stood up and walked back through the thick trees to the road that led back through the fields to town and home.

I did my chores, wood and coal for the kitchen stove, and then I went into the front room and sat by the oil furnace to get warm. The sun by then had just begun to set and the temperature to drop and you could see your breath.

About an hour after dark I heard my brother come in and Mom asked him where he had been and why he was come home so late after dark. Immediately he burst into tears and sobbed out the terrible story. We had gone out to the sand hill to play but some how I had got lost and when they had gathered on the road to come home I wasn't there. They had waited and waited but I had not come. By this time I had figured out that they had not made the circle out to the south but to the north. I had already gone back to town by the time they had gathered at the road so they had not seen me. Bro continued the story. As their concern for me had grown they had courageously gone back into the hills to search the area where I had last been seen and now he wailed I was out in the cold and dark wandering in the woods and I would die out there if I wasn't found soon.

"No he won't," Mom informed him, "David is in the front room sitting by the heater."

Bro had to see with his own eyes the truth of this statement and he came into the front room where I sat. Staring at me with his big tear filled eyes he said,

"Damned you!"

Truth or Consequences

My father taught school in Fillmore which was fifteen miles north of where we lived and my brother went to junior high there; but I went to grade school in my home town. I was in the sixth grade and I was the youngest boy in my family. The school was only two and a half blocks from home so I went home every day for lunch. During the lunch hour it was my job to water the pigs which I did faithfully---except on the days that I was winning marbles at a wonderful rate and I just couldn't break away; but this only happened about five percent of the time.

When it was warm enough to play marbles it was also warm enough for the pigs to want to drink all of their water and tip the trough over long before Dad got home from school. There was really no way for him to know if I watered the pigs or not. Occasionally he would ask me if I had but this very rarely fell on a day that I hadn't so it was *extremely* rare for me to have to lie.

One evening we sat at the dinner table amid all the normal noise created by a family with seven children when Dad asked me if I had watered the pigs. I said that I had and added that they had come over to the trough and slurped it down and I had filled the trough again and gone back to school.

Dad nodded his head indicating he had accepted the report. Ten minutes later, just as information for the family Dad said, "Bill Meinhart came at ten o'clock this morning and took the pigs to the auction." Then he just went on eating.

Years later I had married and begun to raise a family. It was my habit to sit and read in the evenings after it was too dark to work. One evening as I finished a biography of George Washington I laid the book down with a big sigh.

"What's the matter, dear? " my wife asked me.

"I wish I had been a great man like George Washington, admired and respected by all."

"Why, you have talents and abilities that George Washington never dreamed of and you have displayed them with creativity and flare."

"Really?" I prompted.

"Certainly. Why, George Washington couldn't even tell a lie!"

A lot of years have passed since and I have gained a reputation. I can now deal with any person in the whole county and seal the deal with a hand shake. I'm trusted far and wide and it sure has made life a lot easier. You bet, there is nothing like a good reputation for honesty to open doors and smooth the way. Just the other day I had to stop at the dentist's to have a tooth pulled. It was an emergency and I got there just before quitting time. Jon stayed a few extra minutes and did the job. After I got out of the chair I facetiously said, "Jon, you're sure good at extracting teeth but now let's see how good you are at extracting money from me."

Jon turned to Kae, his dental assistant and a girl I had gone to school with and said. "I've never had a minute's trouble getting money out of Dave."

"I wouldn't think so," Kae answered.

"He's got an honest wife!" Jon exclaimed.

No sir, there is nothing like a good reputation if you're going to do business in a small rural community!

Trickery

     I think trickery is one of the essential principles of human survival and has really gotten a bad name. Of course there is the negative side, like all natural law, and it can be used for wicked and immoral ends but it also has a positive side to it. I will attempt to rehabilitate trickery and put it in a proper prospective. Children use it to survive in a world where the "big people" make all the important decisions affecting life, liberty and property. My sister used it to get out of washing the dishes every day at noon. Mom would say "Go practice the piano for fifteen minutes and I will start the dishes. After you are done practicing you come and finish up." So my sister would practice her piano. After each piece she would listen carefully to see if mother was rattling the dishes. If she was then my sister would play some more.

     Usually she could stretch practice time until Mother had finished the dishes, cleaned the table, wiped the cupboard and mopped the floor. The rattling of the dishes would certainly had to have happened in between these other jobs in spaced intervals but Mother just never did catch on to what Linda was doing. I guess subconsciously Mom wanted her to develop the obvious talent she displayed for music. To this day my sister still plays the piano at church and community functions. Just think of all the pleasure that she and her listeners would have missed out on if she hadn't tricked mother into washing the dishes.

When our children were small and the budget got tight my wife and I would invite friends over for a big potluck party. We didn't invite the friends' children and we made sure that our older friends were invited, for the older women were good cooks and they didn't have children to feed at home so they wouldn't want to take a lot of food back home with them; my wife always offered to let our children eat it and she would put the extra food in the refrigerator and wash the dish for the guests. My wife is considerate that way. Of course our children wanted to come and eat all the good food and listen to the adults talk.

Our friends were experts in several areas of expertise but all had an over lapping interest in the several topics. John Adams, named after his illustrious ancestor and namesake was, you guessed it, an expert on the functions of government and constitutional law. Another couple were cooks at the hospital and were very much interested in human nutrition. They didn't think much of institutional food. Another, a truck driver was up on current events. One man was a financial consultant and his wife was an insurance lady. Another couple were into biological research and were experimenting on biological medicine both diagnostic and application. A university level mathematician was counted among our ranks. The conversation was of course lively and any topic could be discussed.

My little children would sit quietly and listen for hours for they knew that if they got sleepy and started to yawn or if they got noisy I would say "What are you doing still up at this late hour?!" and I would send them to bed. They have all done well and all study on their own in their various homes now that they have all grown up. Just think, they might never have taken an interest in a classical liberal education if they had not tricked their parents into letting them stay up way past their bed time.

I hear that Thomas Jefferson listened in on George Wythe and friends while he was supposed to be there just to play the violin. Think of all the world may have missed out on if he hadn't tricked those old men into mentoring him in the philosophy of the founding era. Abraham was tricked into giving Jacob the birthright blessing and Jacob was tricked into starting the House Israel, Adam was tricked into eating the apple and Judah was tricked into starting the line that produced King David, Solomon and Jesus. So you see that trickery has a long and vulnerable history...venerable history.

How to Pick a Watermelon

I never do the shopping in my family except when the watermelons are in season. My wife is always bragging about how I never pick a bad one. It's true that I'm an expert in my field. My children however are always bugging me about my secrets and why I always close my eyes before I thump a melon.

Stories are a good diversion to keep secrets away from children so I always tell about time that Frank and his buddies decided that Harvey's melons were ripe so a couple of hours after dark, when they thought that he would be fast a sleep, they sneaked into his patch. Now Harvey, being an experienced watermelon raiser, figured that it was about time for Frank and his friends to sneak into his patch. About two hours after dark when he normally went to bed he got his shotgun and walked out past his corrals to his vacant lot where the watermelon patch was. About the time that he came through the gate the boys heard him and made a dash to the east side of the patch and were slithering through the fence. Harvey raised his shot gun and fired into the air above their heads.

At the precise moment that Harvey fired, Frank snagged himself good on the barbed wire and tore a gash in his skin and he began to holler.

"George, Bill, Harold, Henry...help me! I've been shot!"

The above story is one of the legends in our little town. I don't know if it is true. I am a generation younger than Frank and I just heard that he died and his funeral is on Wednesday. Harvey of course was a generation older than Frank and he has been gone for forty five years. I guess I'll never know if this is a true story or just a legend but it diverted the children.

My brother was a big, strong kid but he didn't make it when he tried to jump Jack Day's garden fence with a water melon under each arm. Although he got caught he wouldn't rat on his friends so he got to pay the debt to Jack all by himself. He weeded Jack's garden for a day…a farmer's day - daylight to dark.

Another time Bro and his friends harvested more watermelon than they could eat. The remaining melons were dashed to pieces on the cement inside the entrance way to the school house. The next day the principle of the school asked him to help clean it up. Bro felt too guilty to tell him no. They started with shovels, changed to brooms and finally to a garden hose. The place was spic and span by the time the other students got to school. The principle gave Bro a dollar for helping. That was a lot of money in those days and Bro felt guilty about taking it. He didn't feel guilty enough to confess and if he wasn't going to confess he couldn't think up a good reason to refuse the money.

People talk about how safe it used to be to walk the streets at night in our little town. It probably was for adults in those days but it wasn't for little boys. The parents seem oblivious to the fact that there lurked a terrible menace in the shadows of the night.

We little kids marched the streets in our little gangs for fun but mostly for protection. Nothing, not Dracula, not Werewolf, not the Mummy, not Frankenstein, could strike terror into our hearts like the phrase... "There are the big boys!!!" Late one night we were on our way home. Crossing the city park would cut a block off the trip and we were already late. The park wasn't lit like it is today but the same trees are there. We were half way across and already in the shadows of the trees when dark shapes moved! The big boys!!

It was too late, they had already seen us.

"Hey, don't run off. We got some watermelon for you," they called in friendly voices. Sure enough there were several watermelons sitting there on the grass at their feet. They coaxed us over and broke open a melon and offered it to us.

"Just eat the hearts. There are so many, that's all you will have room for. We are already stuffed."

We were still suspicious but we tried the melon and it was delicious. Several watermelon hearts later we too were stuffed and amazed that the big boys had been so nice to us. Reality returned with a vengeance when the big boys took the heartless watermelon halves and jammed them on our heads like beanies and twisted them around using our heads like orange juicers until the rind covered our eyes.

"You are now members of the watermelon club," they told us. "If you take your watermelon crowns off before you get home we will be very offended and we will think you don't want to be members of our club. We would be very hurt and very mad, understand?"

We understood perfectly. We didn't take our crowns off until we were well on our way home and figured they couldn't catch us before we got there.

It must have been a big raid for some of the gardeners thought the problem was past a joke. Of course all the little boys were blamed. There was evidence all over us and all over the park. We protested of course and ratted on the big boys. Nobody would believe us. Blaming our sins on the big boys had nearly always worked before but this time I guess the evidence was too great to ignore… but we were innocent - framed!

The kids always liked these stories about my childhood and they never did figure out why it had to be dark…I mean why I always close my eyes when I pick a watermelon.

Civil Disobedience

The nights were cool but the afternoons were still warm and pleasant enough for the students to sit outside on the grass and enjoy the companionship of lifelong friends. The girls wore dresses to school every day and on special days they even wore girdles and nylons. Mini-skirts were a couple of years in the future. Gloria was a real scandal; she smoked tobacco with the boys sometimes. The boys wore nice slacks and loafers the first day or two of school but then went back to what they were used to, clean Levis and cowboy boots. Football was the most often discussed topic of the conversation right behind who was dating who. John Wayne was a big box office sell as one of the young, handsome movie stars; Doris Day, the envy of all the female population, fresh faced and wholesome. Fifteen year old men experimented with the foul tasting adult beverage called 'ollies.' Teachers and principal discussed the problems of sluffing and gum chewing in faculty meetings. The one or two girls that got pregnant each year quickly married their boyfriends.

Noon hour came to an end when the bell rang and Mrs. Randall's sophomore English class reluctantly left the lawn and the company of their girls and entered the school. Fifteen, going on sixteen, the students were still enchanted and shy by the 'boy meets girl ritual' although they had entered the first grade together all those years past. Built in the Greek style with the large fluted pillars standing guard over the entrance, the school boasted two stories and large windows for natural light that was thought at the time to enhance the learning atmosphere. Mrs. Randall's room was only one door down from the Principal's office, maybe four steps.

The students entered the room at the northwest corner, and sat in any desk they chose except for one boy who had an assigned seat, whose desk butted right up to the teacher's. When both were seated, they sat three feet apart and eyeball to eyeball. The aisle alongside was the only access the boy had to his desk. He was rather quiet, shy around the girls, inarticulate and quite a challenge to the teachers; he day-dreamed all the time. When reminded by the teacher to pay attention, this was usually done by asking him a question, his reply invariably would bring a laugh. No one was quite sure if he was an idiot who didn't know what was going on or if he did it on purpose.

After the students had settled into their seats Mrs. Randall entered. She was a neatly dressed, trim, attractive woman. Her hair, of three colors, from dark to iron gray fading into white was very attractive and obviously done every week at the beauty parlor. She walked briskly in a no nonsense march, straight and proper. She was educated and cultured and was well aware of her social status.

Her age was hard to determine. Any guess from late forties to sixty would be good. Walking quickly to her desk, Mrs. Randall picked up her glasses and then her teacher's manual and prepared to start class; but before she could speak, Sammie, who had been sitting in the middle of the room, got up and proceeded to the pencil sharpener that was situated in the far southeast corner of the room, sharpened her pencil and returned to her seat. Sammie, described as attractive but not one of the popular girls of the class for she was much too timid, sat innocent of the fact that Mrs. Randall was not happy. Mrs. Randall deliberately took off her glasses, laid her manual back down on the desk and stalked over to Sammie's desk. "Samantha, you know full well that the rule in this class is that you sharpen your pencil BEFORE THE SECOND BELL RINGS! Your actions show a blatant disregard of the rules and rudeness unbecoming a young lady, not to mention disrespect to your teacher. I'll not put up with this." By this time, Mrs. Randall had her finger in the poor girl's face. "Your parents will hear of this and there may be other disciplinary action." The moisture that had gathered at the corner of her mouth was later described as a foaming at the mouth, but the students were exaggerating. Sammie was in tears and tried to protest, but Mrs. Randall plunged on. "I have never been interrupted so rudely in all my years here at this . . . . ." The second bell rang. As you may well imagine, the lecture ended immediately but Mrs. Randall merely turned and went back to her desk and, picking up her glasses and manual, prepared once again to start the class.

Snap! The sound of a pencil lead being broken was heard clearly throughout the now deathly quiet room. All eyes, including the teacher's, riveted upon the boy immediately before her desk. He was looking at the lead as it rolled down the slope and onto the floor. His eyes now surveyed the pencil. Everyone in the room knew what he was going to do next. Casually he got up from his seat and walked at his naturally slow pace to the back of the room, his boots with the horseshoe taps, clumped loudly on the wooden floor. Across the back of the room he clumped and then up the east side toward the pencil sharpener. The east side of the room, you will recall, boasted the window. Three feet up from the floor and the whole length of the room, it gave a panoramic view of the front lawn, trees and the building across the street. A bird flew from the north to south and swooped up into the tall pine tree on the corner outside the room. It caught the notice of the boy and he followed it with his eyes and head, to its perch. The first snickers were heard. Reaching his destination, the boy inserted his pencil and began the slow grind. Pulling it out, he examined the point. It was long and tapered but it did not have the little ball on the end that was possible to achieve if one was careful. He inserted it again and ground away. He pulled it out. It had broken off altogether. Again he ground away; again the end was long and tapered but didn't have the ball. Carefully he cranked the handle and finally the pencil came out with the little ball on the end. He smiled. Each action was done in such a manner as to permit everyone to see or know what he was doing. On his clumping, noisy journey back to his seat he looked at the flowers lined up along beneath the window. More snickers. Once back in his seat he put the pencil in its groove at the top of the desk, stretched his feet out in front of him and, crossing his arms in a most comfortable manner, looked up at the teacher. He was ready for class, his pencil was sharp. His eyes were steady and calm, as was his spirit.

Mrs. Randall was forming words with her mouth, her eyebrows in a deep scowl over furious eyes; her hand bringing her glasses up to her face was trembling. Now free of the glasses her hand came down in a chopping movement with finger extended, mimicking the motion when she was scolding Sammie but no words escaped her mouth. The glasses came off again but now the teeth were clenched and the mouth in a hard line. Like a spasm, the glasses went back on and came off and were tossed onto the desk. Staccato hammering of high heels on hard wood broke the silence as Mrs. Randall made a beeline for the door, which she flung open. Before the air pressure in the compressed air door stop permitted the door to close, the students saw the door to Mr. Wright's office jerked open. Yes, Mrs. Randall's husband was the Principal.

As soon as the door is safely closed, the kids burst out laughing except for the boy in the assigned seat. He looks at the others a bit puzzled. They laugh harder. Nobody leaves their seats but the buzz of conversation is continuous. Mr. Randall is a retired army Colonel and has been the Principal for many years. Although the boys make fun of him they know he puts up with no nonsense. Friendly and diplomatic as he is, no one can mistake the swift march led by his jutting chin. Blood is expected to run in the aisles and none of the students want to be found out of his seat or out of line. Time passes slowly. The suspense builds. What can Principal and Mrs. Randall be planning? Speculation abounds but the boy in the condemned seat sits silent. The class period now is almost gone, the class subdued.

Once again the door is flung open and Mrs. Randall marches in. Her face is set in iron. Marching once again to her desk, she puts on her glasses with steady fingers and, opening her book, she reads tomorrow's assignment in a clear, calm voice. Once this is done she leaves in the same manner and disappears once more into her husband's office. There is no laughter now, no visiting, only the rustling of papers as the students look up their assignment in their books. It is a big one but there are no groans or protests. The bell rings. Only the muffled sounds of books and papers can be heard as the students gather up their possessions, and quietly and orderly, leave the room.

Innocent

As we were talking about our childhood an old friend made the comment that I never got into trouble. By that he meant that I never got caught and he ask me how I managed because, if he remembered right, I was right in the middle of most of the mischief that went on in our little town in those days. Those days were the late fifties and early sixties. Mischief was comprised of doing stuff like stealing gooseberries. By the way that reminds me of the time we were sitting in the vacant lot next to Rob's house in the dark with our salt and soda and his gooseberries. The night was warm and there was no moon but the stars were ablaze. Somehow Rob detected the fact that the kids were into his bushes…again and he came out the back door and hollered at us. Of course we jumped up and in a closely packed herd ran for the gate in front of the vacant house. I knew the boys were going to run out the front gate and down the street where they wouldn't trip and fall. I also knew that Rob would jump in his car and catch them and they would all get in trouble.

He would catch them but not me. I veered off from the pack and went behind the house. I would go to the back of the vacant lot and out onto the street and go the opposite direction from the rest and arrive home safe and sound. Events followed just as I had them figured out in my mind, however there was one event I had not anticipated. Have you ever been clothes lined? I mean literally clotheslined? I couldn't see it in the dark and I was moving at a pretty good clip when the next thing I knew I was parallel with the ground at about five feet. My head had abruptly stopped but the rest of me kept going at least for a very short distance. Of course the fall was straight down and flat on the back.

While the rest of the boys were being caught I was rolling around on the ground in the weeds making choking noises. I don't know if it was the wire across the throat or the blow on the back that knocked the breath out of me. You might say that I got my form of punishment but I didn't get caught!

It was a little late on Sunday morning when I got up and wandered into the kitchen where mom was crisping a piece of toast. I had been gone for a couple of nights staying with a friend from another town. After saying good morning mom asked me what I had done the night before.

"Well first of all we got in Peck's old car and headed for Delta (a town about forty miles away) but on the way we hit a cloud burst and a huge puddle on the road. It knocked the muffler off his car so it was really loud when you accelerated or geared down. Once in Delta we bought some beer and got drunk and picked up some girls but soon thereafter their boy friends got after us and chased us down. We won the fight but lost the girls. The cops got after us. I don't know if it was the fight that had been reported or if it was the loud car but we ditched them by driving down by the flumes and hiding in the brush. We got stuck in the mud. I lost my shoe in the mud. We walked back to Delta and stayed at John's sister's house and the next morning we walked over to John's Delta girl friend's house and borrowed her father's tractor and went and pulled the car out of the mud and found my shoe. Peck's car threw a rod on the way home and we hitch hiked over to John's place and he brought me home in his father's car."

Of course I told her all this with a little smile on my face and a twinkle in my eye.

"What did you really do?" she asked.

"We went to the movie in Fillmore."

"That's what I thought." She smiled at me fondly.

I always like to give Mom a chance to pick the story she likes best. By the way, the names have been changed to protect the guilty. They haven't all died yet. The statutes of limitations have run out long ago but this is a very small town and...It's just wise to play the cards close to the chest I always say.

No, I was never officially connected to the bombing of the girls with cherry bombs in overripe melons. My name wasn't ever associated with the fire crackers in green walnut husks thrown down Miller's furnace vent. It wasn't me caught red handed putting sheep on the school bus on

Halloween. Mrs. Anderson and Mrs. Jensen could never understand when Kim and Jules rolled their eyes when they said, "Why can't you be like Dave, he never gives his mother a minutes trouble."

Of course after all these years I've become a responsible and upright citizen. I just don't understand why my wife . . . We were sitting in Sunday school when the teacher said that the only things we take into the next life with us will be our knowledge and our character. My wife pipes right up and says,

"I can understand why I would want to keep my knowledge but what would I do with my character?" and she looked at me significantly.

Point of View

In my younger years I was accident prone. It started about the time that I entered school and lasted until I had a good start into adulthood. There are differing opinions as to why this happened. Early during first grade I was racing my older brother out to the corral and the loser had to milk the cow. I was only six and didn't know how to milk the cow but it created a challenge. Bro was a big strong lad of about fourteen. I got the jump on him and was out in front but he soon began to pass me. A plan came into my mind. I would throw a side body block on him and knock him down, then I would jump up and win the race. After all he was only about three times my size. The block was quite effective and he went sprawling, hit the ground and went sliding through the grass just as I had planned. I didn't plan the part where I would be under him… broken collar bone. My dad put me in the car and took me to the hospital.

The next year roller skating became a big thing amongst the younger set and we would get together and play "hockey" down at the open-air dance hall. The only place to practice my skating at home was the front porch. It wasn't that big and as I would go round and round I would have to make a lot of sharp turns for if I didn't there was the two foot drop to the ground or worse onto the sidewalk.

It was great practice and I became very mobile on my skates. But, as my confidence grew, the faster I went and the sharper the turns. As you have probably guessed by now I got too close to the edge and one skate went over throwing me off the porch onto the side walk...broken wrist. My dad put me in the car and took me to the hospital.

Soon to follow was the box elder willow spear in the eye. I wasn't blinded but there was a lot of blood and ...well my dad put me in the car and took me to the hospital. One of the most painful accidents was when I burned the back of my legs and had to spent Easter vacation and many other days lying on my face while mother put soothing salve on me. Of course we made the trip to the hospital in the car. Dad drove.

The time I got shot in the foot Dad didn't drive me to the hospital. We did everything we could to keep him from knowing about it but of course it was futile. But that is a story for a different time. Let me list a few other accidents not necessarily in order; three broken ribs, a brain concussion, the garden rake driven through my foot, the fall off the front of a fast moving car (I removed the last piece of gravel from my arm one year later) the knife through the hand, the electrocution, and the poisoning. Did I mention the bout with Hodgkin's disease? The last was not an accident but I was terribly ill and had to suffer the pain of operations but through the blessings of heaven my recover was complete and I haven't had a re occurrence in over thirty five years. After my father died the endings to my stories changed from "My father put me in the car and took me to the hospital," to "My friends thought I was dead."

Different members of the family have different explanations for why I have suffered so many of the pains and agonies of life. My brothers leaned toward stupidity, Mom and a sister liked to think I had a valuable mission to perform in life but my twelve year old son came up with an explanation that my children favor. One night after hearing me tell all these stories he sat silent for a few minutes then quietly said, "You can't kill a man that was born to hang."

High Drama

I may have mentioned in one of my other essays that I got shot in the foot. Jon, my brother's friend, had come to stay the weekend with us. His family lived only twenty-five miles away so he went to the same high school with us. Of course Bro wanted to show him a good time so he talked Dad into letting us take our older brother's car out on the desert to hunt rabbits. The thing wasn't licensed and Bro didn't have a driver's license either. Dad told us to drive out the lane and in no circumstance were we to go near Main Street where the cop would see us. Of course we promised up and down to be strictly obedient. We couldn't find any rabbits, or too few to keep us entertained, so when we found ourselves about 26 miles west of town near Taft's desert cabin we stopped to investigate. There was a corral for the sheep herders to keep their horses close at night, the cabin itself, which was no more than a sheep camp and the tack shed-granary combination.

Finally we found game! Dozens of mice were in the grain bin eating to their hearts content. Being two years younger than Bro and his two friends, Jake and Jon it was natural for me to be at the tale end of the line and I stopped near the east end of the bin and began blazing away with my twenty-two caliber rifle. Bro, Jake and I were all raised in the country and we slaughtered mouse after mouse but Jon having recently moved in from the city found his aim centered on an already dead mouse each time. Finally we were down to the last terrified mouse that was racing around the bin like a mad man. We generously let Jon shoot him.

"I got him!" he cried.

As Jon made his last and only successful shot I felt a heavy blow on the instep of my right foot and looking down I saw the small hole in my boot as it slowly filled with blood.

I elbowed my bro in the ribs and said in a calm and normal voice.

"I've been shot."

He didn't believe me.

"If you'd been shot you wouldn't be standing there so calm! Who are you trying to trick now."

"No, look." I said and pointed to the bleeding boot.

"Dave's been shot!" he yelled pointing at my foot.

The rifles were handed to Jon, and Bro and Jake each grabbed an arm and flung it over their shoulders like they had seen the cowboys in the movies do it and ran me toward the car with Jon bringing up the rear with the weapons. They put me in the back seat with Jon and they climbed in the front.

Bro spun the tires and we went streaking up the dirt road throwing dust and gravel into the fall air. Curves and corners were taken in long slides and fish tails. Bro's eyes were concentrating on the road ahead and his hands were white knuckled on the wheel.

Jon was the epitome of disconsolation.

"I shot him! I shot him!" he moaned over and over again as he rocked back and forth. Finally Jake observed,

"Look how calm he is!"

It was true I was as calm as could be. The blow to my foot had numbed it and I could hardly feel a thing. I'd suffered enough accidents to know that I wasn't seriously hurt. The speed picked up as we hit the straighter road as we neared town. The dust ceased to billow out behind us as we started onto the paved road. Two blocks later we stopped at the stop sign at Main Street. Bro was in such a panic to get me to the hospital that we might not have stopped at all if it hadn't been for the tractor coming around the corner. It was Dad on his way down the lane to his farm. Of course he stopped.

"What in the Sam Hill are you doing on Main Street?! I distinctly told you not to cross Main Street and here you are! Now turn that thing around and get your "t-other-ends" for home!"

This was all said in a very loud voice accompanied by that look that we knew well. Bro turned the car around and headed for home but we stopped at the neighbor's. The lady was a widow but her oldest son was sixteen and had a license and he agreed to take me to the hospital, which was fifteen miles away. On the way it was decided to take me to the doctor's office on Main Street where I was likely to get attention quicker. Their imaginations had run away with them by the time they got there. Being now four in number each took hold of a limb and literally hauled me across the lawn, through the door and up the stairs to the doctor's office. Some friends passing by saw me being carried in this manner and thought I was dead. I was so embarrassed.

The Doctor did drop whatever else he was doing and attended to me. They laid me on an examination table and showed Doc the blood filled hole in my boot. Jake whipped out the hunting knife he carried in his belt and said.

"Do you want me to cut his boot off, Doc?"

"No, we will just slip it off," which he did.

The spent lead had penetrated the boot, the sock and my foot but had not broken the sock on the other side and was lodged there inside it. We figured that the lead must have killed the mouse, traveled through three or four inches of grain, and while perforating the board on the end of the bin hit a knot, ricocheted out at a forty-five degree angle and hit my foot. The hole was fairly clean with only a few bone chips in it. The Doctor put a drain in it and told me to come back in three days and he would check the wound and remove the drain. He then wrapped the wound in a little gauze and tape to hold it in place. I put the boot back on and walked back out to the car and they drove me home.

Meanwhile the neighbor lady had called Mom and Dad and told them what had happened and they were sitting in the front room waiting when we got there. The boys, including myself, were pretty nonchalant about the whole thing now that they understood how minor the wound really was. I played basketball that night. And of course they wanted to play down the whole incident for the folks. I'm guessing they felt pretty sheepish at their extreme reaction for none of them ever mentioned it again. But I know one thing; Bro was very successful in his efforts to show his friend an exciting weekend.

Sneak Attack

There is no recollection of how it all began but I found myself in guerrilla warfare with my good buddy Phil. He was bigger and stronger than I. In fact he was quite a strong and husky built kid about my same height. I, on the other hand, was built more on the slender side…aright, I was skinny but I was quick and agile and could easily outrun him. This warfare was carried on at high school which is about the only place I ever saw him, for he lived in a different town. There are six or eight little towns that gather at the bigger central town where the high school is. After we were old enough to drive we got around much more but in our fifteenth year we were pretty much at the mercy of school busses and parents to get around.

Our warfare consisted mainly in ambush. Of course the planning of the ambush was easier for me because I could simply jump out of some tiny nook and punch him and run away and he couldn't catch me. On the other hand he had to have a bigger hiding place and he had to have a refuge that he could dart into before I recovered enough to be in pursuit, but he managed quite well. This had been going on for about two weeks and I had executed the perfect ambush on Phil just the day before so I was being very wary, expecting to be assaulted from any side at any moment; but since we were in shop class in a room that was big and wide that offered no concealment I was at my ease.

Out of nowhere came the heavy blow to my arm that knocked me off balance. By the time I got my feet back under me and whirled Phil had ten steps on me and was headed to the short hallway that led to the lavatory and wash up room. Even in that short space he barely got the door closed before I hit it. Now this door was a full two inches thick of solid wood and swung inside of the cleanup room, the handle being on the inside. With his foot braced against the bottom of the door and his hands holding the handle and with his superior weight and size I could not push the door open.

Quickly seeing that brute strength wasn't working I settled on another plan. The hallway that led to the cleanup room was about seven feet in width and although the door was also very wide there was a space to the side of it where one couldn't be seen through the little high window in the big door. I pushed for a while to let Phil know I had put forth a big effort to get him but had finally seen it was futile then I flatten myself against the wall out of sight. Right on schedule his face appeared in the window and moved around trying to see into every corner. After a brief time to reassure himself, he would cautiously come out and I planned to whirl around and punch him in the stomach, which we usually didn't do. I really didn't want to seriously hurt him so I was going to hold up at the last minute but still let him know that we were even. He had hit me really hard this time.

Sure enough the door creaked open and he came out but instead of coming cautiously, he marched right out and I didn't have time to temper the punch but gave it to him full force. My fist sinking into a large soft pillow clean to the wrist was the first indication that I had hit someone other than my firm bodied athletic friend. Even as my fist sank deep, I looked up into the face of Mr. B. the older bus driver from another town. His eyes were screwed tight shut from the pain and his lips in a fine 0 were blowing out every bit of air in him -whoosh! Instantly I was gone. What seemed like an eternity later but could not have been five minutes Mr. B. emerged from the cleanup room hallway and stood looking over the class. He had tears in his eyes. Like all the other boys I was busy measuring and cutting on a piece of wood. Finally, not being able to finger the culprit, Mr. B. left. As soon as he was gone Phil emerged from the hallway also and he too had tears in his eyes and he acted like his stomach hurt him but I think his problems were mirth induced. We decided that we had better call a truce before we got in trouble or somebody got hurt…I mean before somebody else got hurt.

And don't worry about me getting in trouble now for Mr. B. has been in the grave for a number of years.

Boss

The boss says that the costumer is always right but the employee knows that the boss is always right especially in those businesses where neither the boss nor the employee works directly with the public. A friend of mine, being the only son of a rich cattle man moved to Nevada to run a cattle ranch of his own. He was now the boss. One day an old cow that had just been separated from her calf was on the prod and had run the cowboys out of the corral. She was a rather skinny, bony old thing and had never been dehorned. These aforementioned head ornaments were curved forward and were wide and sharp. She would shake her head, whirling her weaponry about in the air in a fiercely intimidating manner.

"What's the matter, boys?" the boss chided, "You're not afraid of an old cow are you?"

"She's pretty mean."

"You just have to let her know whose boss." And so saying the boss got into the corral. No sooner was he on the ground the old gal charged. Calmly he stood his ground and when she was near he waved his hat and confidently hollered, "Hey, get outta here, ya old bitch."

Only the fact that the cow charged straight on saved him. Each horn, close on each side of his body, chipped a hunk of wood out of the fence.

Quickly backing up a few feet the cow tipped her head to remedy the oversight of the first charge. She came at him again. This time he was saved by the cowboys on the top of the fence who jerked him up out of harms way milliseconds before the horn chipped the fence right where he had been standing.

Two miles to the northeast of town a local resident set up a feed lot. He already owned the acreage necessary to raise the feed for the animals. One day it was discovered that an underground irrigation pipe had broken. Of course it would have to be excavated and repaired. This was in the days before he could afford a back hoe so the digging would have to be done by a crew with shovels. The ground was wet but not mucky. One big strong man thrust his shovel in and pried back on it to remove the first shovelful to start the job. The ground did not give way as he expected but the shovel handle snapped cleanly off.

"Any damn fool can break a shovel handle!" the boss cried and grabbing a shovel from one of the other worker he thrust it into the ground and pulled back on it, breaking the handled cleanly off. "See?"

His rent was due and his savings were nearly gone and he was far from home when the farm boy finally landed a good paying job, $1.85 an hour, down at the piano factory. He was assigned to catch the glued panels as they came out of the industrial sized plane and stack them on a cart. When the cart was full he wheeled the panels to the next station where they were cut to a more precise size needed for the pianos. The work was lighter physically than what he was used to but it was also much more boring than anything he had ever done before. He even had to wear huge ear muffs that eliminated any conversation he might have had with co-workers.

The second day on the job about mid-morning a groove appeared in the panels as they came through the plane. He waved at the operator to stop and then pointed out the flaw as he had been instructed to do the day before. After studying the groove for a minute the operator went back to the plane and attempted to adjust it. After the adjustment the next panel still had the groove. Again the machine was shut down and the operator looked it over trying to figure out the problem. The farm boy curiously looked over his shoulder. He didn't understand the adjustment nor what the operator was attempting to do but now as the operator turned the cylinder that held the blades in place the boy noticed a screw that held one of the many blades in place was loose and it corresponded with the groove on the panel.

"That screw is loose," he said and pointed it out with his finger.

"So?" the operator said.

"The centrifugal force pushes the screw up and it cuts the groove," the boy explained.

"I've run this machine since the plant opened and it's never done that before."

Several adjustments and trials later the operator goes and gets the machinist. After several tries by the machinist the problem in not fixed. The boy points out the loose screw and explains to the machinist why the loose screw is cutting the groove in the panels. The machinist merely looks at the boy and waits for him to go sit down which he does.

After lunch the operator and machinist sit down together and read the manual. Every adjustment is made according to specks and still the groove mars every panel. Finally they give up and call in the shop foreman, a man with forty years experience with such machinery. He asks questions and repeats all the previously adjustments but the panel comes out grooved. Again the boy points out the loose screw and explains how it causes the groove. The shop foreman points to the cart that holds the panels and says "Go sit down!"

The three men spend the next hours pouring over the manual and the machine but nothing will eliminate the groove. It's after four o'clock when the foreman reaches up with his screw driver and tightens the screw and orders another panel to be sent through the plane. A smoother, cleaner panel never went though the factory. All three look up to see if the boy had observed their actions that solved the problem but he was carefully looking the other way. A short time later the boy was fired.

Scrooge

My cousin's oldest boy has Downs syndrome and he and I are good friends. He overheard my wife call me Scrooge one Christmas time about twenty five years ago and he has called me Scrooge ever since. My farm is down the lane about a block outside the city limits and my cousin's house is just a block beyond that. It is not unusual while I am working on the farm to hear "Scrooge" yelled at me from the passing car or pickup. I, in turn, have named him Marler after Scrooge's friend. He hollers "Scrooge" and I holler "Marler" then he calls me Marler and I call him Scrooge and so it goes back and forth until he is out of range.

You were probably wondering why my wife was calling me Scrooge in the first place but I can assure you that it was said facetiously. These were the circumstances.

Every Tuesday night I played chess with Bill and the cousin I mentioned above out at Bill's house on the north edge of town. The winner would play until he was defeated then the new champion would stay at the board until he in turn lost. This tournament went on for weeks if not months and I'm not bragging when I say that I spent more time at the board then the other two.

At home I taught the kids to play but all I had for a chess board was a flimsy paste board thing. It had the different colored squares so what did I care, but my wife thought that I should have something nicer. She got with my niece who was living around the corner with her grandmother, my mother, at the time and they decided to get me a new chess board for Christmas. The niece was taking a wood shop class in high school and needed a project to get a grade. The wife agreed to pay for materials. It was the perfect set up for them both. The dark squares of the board were to be made of dark walnut and the light squares of the lightest maple. Each square would be hand crafted to the perfect size then carefully glued together. It was one of the niece's very first projects and things didn't go well but finally the board was ready just before Christmas.

Of course this was a top secret project and only the two of them knew about it. I had seen them with their heads together and suspected that they were making plans for my Christmas but even I didn't have a clue of what it could be. I drove a freight truck in those days and delivered general freight in the area and traveled about 250 miles a day. By some strange coincidence I received a shipment for the high school the last day they were in session before the holidays and when I went to the front desk they determined that the thing went to the wood shop. I was to make arrangements with the shop teacher to get the freight unloaded. I don't remember what it was but it was heavy and the shop students were enlisted to get it off the truck.

While I was waiting for the shop teacher to get things organized I over heard one of the boys mention the beautiful chessboard the redheaded girl from the other class had made. The moment the words were out of his mouth I knew what I was getting for Christmas. December 23rd rolled around and it was our regular chess night but Bill had gone out to California to spend Christmas with his family, so we had canceled for the week. But when the wife asked if I was going to play chess I said, "I'm so sick of chess I could puke. Those guys aren't a bit of competition and I get bored and sleepy and once in a while they get lucky and beat me, then they brag all over town. They never mention all the times I beat them. I don't care if I ever play another game of chess in my whole life!"

The wife was pretty quiet the rest of the evening as was the niece who was there when I declared my intention to never play chess again. Mom and the niece came over early Christmas morning to watch the little kids open their presents. Last of all I got my present and when I opened it there was the beautifully checkered solid wooden chess board with a hard, wear forever shiny finish.

"I know it's not what you wanted but we didn't have time to get you something else," the wife apologized.

"What do you mean? It is just what I wanted and it is beautiful. It must have taken hours and hours to make. Thank you very much"

"But you said you were sick of chess so we thought…" The niece began but by then I had lost control and had started to laugh.

"How did you know?" the wife demanded. "We never told anyone and we didn't even bring it into the house until after you went to bed last night and I know you didn't get up during the night."

"I have my ways," is all I would say.

Anyway, now you know why I was being called Scrooge when my Cousin and his family came over to see us later in the week and why his son calls me Scrooge to this day.

Nickels

He was in first grade when his friend offered to take him to the store on the way home from school and buy him a treat. His friend had a dime and a nickel and he was to choose which coin he wanted. This was in the days when a dime bought a soda and a nickel a candy bar or bag of peanuts. Not wanting to appear greedy the boy chose the nickel. His friend asked him why and he replied, "Because it is bigger."

The next day the friend, with the other boys of the class, once again offered the choice of a dime and a nickel and again the boy took the nickel because it was bigger. The boys got a good laugh out of that. Whenever they wanted a sport they would offer the ignorant boy his choice of coins for a treat. It was especially fun to have new kids in school see how dumb this boy was. After nearly the whole first grade had passed the boy's older brother happened to see the spectacle and after the other boys left asked his little brother "Why do you let them make fun of you like that? You know a dime is worth more than a nickel." The reply came.

"The first time I choose the dime they won't do it any more."

Mark was always complaining to Boyd and Ron down at the cheese plant that he always got stuck with the homely and plump when he and his friends picked up the girls. One day while they were busy at work the most beautiful girl came in and asked for Boyd. She visited with him briefly, touched him on the arm so affectionately and her eyes calm and full of love conveyed the depth of their relationship. Gracious and interested she focused her total attention on Mark and Ron when they were introduced. Again when her visit was over she looked each in the eye and expressed her pleasure at meeting them and they felt like she truly meant it.

Once she was gone Mark stood looking after her with the most wistful look on his face.

"Boyd, how do you catch a girl like that?"

"I don't know?" Boyd answered.

"Oh, come on. I know you were all-state basketball in Idaho. You must have dated all kinds of pretty girls. Give me some pointers!"

"I don't have a clue. My fiancée and I met in the first grade and have been in love ever since. I have never learned how to chase women. I've never done it."

"I wish that had happened to me," Mark was still looking the way she had gone.

"Ron, you date a lot. How does a man get a beautiful girlfriend?"

"Tell me about the last time you picked up the girls and you had to sit in back while your buddy got the pretty one."

"It's always like that. What's to tell?"

"Tell me about the pretty girl. Why do the guys like her?"

"She is fun, outgoing, and smart. She has a nice sense of humor and laughs a lot. She likes to flirt and tease and is just a lot of fun. She's sexy too."

"Sounds like you have observed her very carefully." Ron said. "Why do you think there are always girls like the one you were with, with the one you wanted to be with?"

"Murphy's law?"

Boyd laughed but Ron continued.

"Think about it. This is a friend that the pretty girls invite to sleep-overs eat pizza with, do home work with, and any and all girl things. They love her and want for her all the successes of life. They want her to have fun and have boy friends and to be happy. They want her approval and her love. She is a valued friend. What do you think the pretty girl thinks when you ignore her friend or treat her second rate?"

"Gee I never thought of that?"

"And what would the pretty girl think if you treated her close friend like a real and valuable person rather than "I got stuck with the homely again." Try concentrating on the friend and you will find why the other girls value her so much. You will find she is fun and interesting and you will like her too. She then will tell all the girls that you are wonderful guy and after a while the reputation will spread and old Mark will find the girl he wants along with many new friends."

Only a few short months passed by and Mark was walking down the aisle with a girl that he was very much in love with.

Discipline

Evan moved to our little town about a dozen years ago. We have a lot in common and it wasn't long until we had become good friends. Three or four years ago he introduced me to a friend that had come to church with him. He introduced me in this manner, "This is Dave. I've told you about his children who have done exceptional well, especially in their education."

The friend asked, "Why do you think his children are so exceptional?"

Evan turned toward me and, placing his hand on my arm, looked up into my face. The friend did also and I could see the respect and admiration in his eyes. I stood a little taller and I couldn't help the feeling of pride that began welling up inside. Evan turned back to his friend and said, "They have a wonderful mother!"

Despite some of Evans other traits he is an honest man. My wife is a wonderful mother and the major part of the responsibility of educating our children has fallen upon her shoulders.

I have made some observations of my own that I think might be helpful to parents. Before the student can benefit from a classical education he must learn self-discipline. Self-discipline starts however with other discipline. That is the role of parents and teachers. In this relationship there are five things that CANNOT be tolerated. These are; lying, whining, tantrums, and irrational and unreasonable behavior. Once a parent or teacher has learned not do these things he is ready to discipline a child or student.

You laugh. Maybe I should delve into this a little further. I will tell a short story that includes all these elements.

My father was a school teacher-farmer and every morning before school he got up at five in the morning to do the chores. This consisted of milking seven or eight cows, feeding the cows, the calves, the pigs, and the horses. Two hours work was required for one person to complete the work but my brother Charlie was a big strong teen-age lad and he was assigned to help. The typical morning went like this.

"Charlie, time to get up…Get up, Charlie… Come on Charlie…"

"You go get started, Dad, I'll be right out."

Dad goes out to start the chores and Charlie goes back to sleep and dreams that he is getting up and putting on his clothes and is outside doing the chores. Suddenly water is dashing into his face and he wakes up sputtering. He runs out and milks the two cows that Dad has left for him. He races back to the house and gulps his breakfast and chases the bus down to the store. He usually catches it because the bus drives around the town to get all the kids and Charlie goes cross country.

Charlie defends such behavior like this, "Getting out of a nice warm bed in the middle of the night to go out into the dark, the cold and the snow to milk a bunch of cows is contrary to natural law." We were on vacation somewhere and we were behind schedule and were not going to get home until eleven so Dad called home and told Charlie that he was expected to do the chores. Thirty minutes before chore time his friends came by and said, "Charlie, let's go to Richfield."

"I can't, I have to do the chores." Charlie answered.

"Come on, we'll help you do the chores when we get home. We won't be late."

And because Charlie could resist anything but temptation he got in the car and went to Richfield. One thirty in the morning his friends get him back home where the house is dark and all is quiet. Now, the typical chain of events is that Dad having arrived home at eleven and seeing that the chores were not done would do them and go to bed. The next day he would lose his temper and kick Charlie's "t-other-end".

Moving quietly so as to not disturb anyone Charlie walked around to the back door and just as he was reaching to open it, it opened and a hand was thrust out with a milk bucket in it. Not a word was spoken, but Charlie took the bucket and did the chores.

Now let's analyze the story according to the five don'ts of discipline. First of all, the typical reaction of my father was to do the chores himself. Or in other words he lied. He didn't expect Charlie to do the chores - he wanted him to do the chores and he hoped he would do the chores but he didn't expect him to do the chores. Second he whined. Now, I never heard my father whine. It just wasn't his personality but I'll bet he did on occasion look toward heaven and say, "Why me Lord? What have I done to deserve this?" The tantrum was expressed by losing his temper and kicking Charlie's t-other end. This was done with the side of the foot and really didn't hurt but one could feel the power and this coupled with the expression on Dad's face could be quite intimidating. But Charlie had learned that this discomfort only lasted for two seconds and he had exchanged this for two hours work he didn't have to do and eight hours of fun with his friends. Charlie was a reasonable and rationale person. Dad on the other hand thought that two seconds of stress would deter Charlie's irresponsible behavior. You must call this irrational and unreasonable behavior.

Now the next time the boys came by and said, "Let's go to Richfield" and Charlie had the chores to do, he declined to go even when they said they would help with the chores when they got back. "What's gotten into you Charlie?" they asked.

He answered, "My father has become honest and reasonable and rational."

"Oh, no!"

They thought of everything they could to get around this obstacle but it was no use. Not even the

NAATP (National Association for the Advancement of Teenage People) could help. Their challenge was even greater than they supposed because that didn't know, as did Charlie's Dad, that Charlie was afraid of the dark. If Charlie was here he would defend himself and say that he was not afraid of the dark—He was afraid of what was in the dark. These nuances are crucial to the story, I think. In the face of all the difficulties, seen and unseen, there was nothing to do but help Charlie do the chores before they left.

Another subsection of the above principles are threats. Threats are almost useless. If you threaten a child with bodily harm and he is disobedient then he has trapped you into being a felon or a liar. Most parents chose to be liars and do the chores in the middle of the night. Another dire threat that is common is, "If you do that one more time I will ground you until you are thirty-five!" This can only be effective if you can show the object of the threat a letter from the Pope showing his support for the legal age limit being raised to the above mentioned number, campaign plans from the political action committee promoting the same on government stationary under the signature of the Governor's wife and the Supreme Court decisions leaning in that direction but don't feel completely sure of your ground until you get him to watch the panel, made up of the Governor's wife, the Pope and the Chief Justice of the Supreme Court, discussing the inevitability of the age of majority being raised to thirty-five, on the Oprah Winfrey show.

The only alternative to these two examples is to control the tongue, do not lie, and act in a rational and reasonable manner. In place of threats, have rules that exclude cruel and unusual punishment, exclude hearsay, confessions can be used against him only if made in open court, and punishment is known and is administered equitably. If administered fairly several things will result; You don't lie to each other, each acts in reasonable and rational ways, threats are not needed and are done away with, order abounds and respect and love grows between the parent and child, the teacher and student, the chores get done in the daylight and if the parent or teacher has a relapse at least he has introduced the element of unpredictability and uncertainty into the equation.

This is called the Russian Roulette principle. The parent's success rate increases in direct proportion to the number of chambers he is able to keep loaded, but again it's best to keep a fully loaded gun.

Negotiation is a good tool if understood in its proper place. The Authority of the parent is not negotiable. You ask what this means. Mommy wants junior to eat breakfast but junior doesn't want to come to the table. "Come on, dear so we can clean up the dishes and go downtown." Junior plops down on the floor. "Here, I'll put your eggs in your favorite bowl." Junior rolls over and bawls. "Would you rather have just one egg?" Junior rolls over and kicks his feet. "Now don't be that way, the whole family is waiting for you." Junior bucks, kicks and bawls. Negotiations continue as long as mom permits it and junior is getting what he wants, which might be attention or the possibility of getting sugary cereal instead of eggs or any other unknown desire that mommy is supposed to guess.

Let's try that again. Mommy serves breakfast but junior doesn't want to come to the table. The family eats and begins to clear the table in preparation to a trip downtown. In a panic, junior starts to negotiate for his breakfast but the schedule proceeds as planned. Later Mommy serves lunch and junior makes a beeline for the table.

Trickery is one of the best principles to teach a child or student the classics. At our house if a child was acting unpleasant and grumpy he was told to "Go to your room until you can act happy." The more gregarious would in a short time come out of their room and act happy. These children grew up to be happy and pleasant people. The children that liked peace and quiet would go to their rooms and read, sometimes for a long time. These too would come out of their rooms in due time and grew to be happy, pleasant people and good scholars. This works only if there is no television in the room but there are many good and interesting books.

One day I came home from work for lunch and my wife was beginning to put lunch on the table with several hungry children underfoot. She was a little short with them and she didn't have a happy face. I suggested facetiously that maybe she should go to her room until she could act happy. "Thank you, oh, thank you!" She exclaimed and throwing her arms around my neck she kissed me then ran upstairs to her room. I was left to finish putting lunch on the table. I only tell this experience to show that parent/child teacher/student relationships are not to be tried on spouses with any predictable results.

After all the above has met with some degree of success the student can then be introduced to the concepts of self education in the "classical-liberal" tradition.

Feminism

Years ago when my wife and I were first married we moved into a little house that had but four rooms but since we were planning to have a family we decided that we should build on. The wash room, mud room and shower was to be on the west side of the house but since we were not going to put the waste water down the cesspool we decided to dig a drain field out into the middle of the lawn. This would entail a trench about twelve feet long and four feet deep out to the hole that would be about six feet in diameter and six or seven feet deep. We didn't have any money so I would do all the work myself. Shovel work, no back hoe. I started early in the morning and by noon had the trench dug. I was young and ambitious in those days.

After a long afternoon of digging I had the hole about four and a half feet deep. The sun was hot and I was tired so when the wife brought out a large glass of cold lemonade I sat on the edge of the hole to drink it.

"Want me to dig a while?" the wife asked.

"Sure."

She hopped down in the hole and just as she was throwing out the second shovel full of dirt the DOT crew just getting off work drove by.

"Way to go, Dave!" Lynn called.

"That's the way to train 'em!'" - Cecil

"Go, Dave, go!" - Leonard.

"What an example, Dave!"

What could I say? I just raised my glass and saluted them.

My wife is a sensuous woman.

It was hot. We had had a rain shower that afternoon and cooled things off a little but the sun came out and the temperature climbed up near the century mark. Usually in the desert the temperature drops after sun down but it must have clouded up again because it just got muggy. We were still young and poor and couldn't afford air conditioning. Well, nobody had air conditioning in those days unless you were from the city. Anyway, we were laying there suffering through the night but not sleeping 'cause it was just too doggone hot. About two in the morning the wife asked, "How does a big cold glass of ice water sound to you?"

"Great!"

"Since-you-is up will you get me one too?"

My son informed us that he was engaged to be married and I sat him down to give him a little fatherly advice. Among the gems of wisdom I imparted to him was this; "Son, a few polite words will make your marriage go smoother."

"I know how to say 'Please' and 'Thank you'…"

"That's 'Yes, Ma'am' and 'No Ma'am.'" my wife called in from the kitchen.

Our regular routine began before dawn. My wife would fix breakfast while I went outside to milk the cows and feed the animals. One morning I noticed that after I had put my winter clothes on she was still in bed so I thought I'd have a little fun. I went into the bedroom and spoke to her somewhat impatiently,

"Where's my breakfast?!"

Seeing me in my chore clothes she of course figured she had overslept. She leaped out of bed and ran into the kitchen and began to bang the pots and pans around in her rush to get my breakfast on the table before I had to go to work. In the middle of all this I walked over and, picking up the clean milk bucket, I walked out to do the chores.

A while later she put my breakfast on the table before me.

"I'm sorry I burned your pancakes," she smiled sweetly.

I laughed and ate my burned pancakes and went to work. I had had my fun and she had had hers and we were even, right? No harm done.

"Oh, I forgot, you don't like split pea soup do you?" she smiled sweetly at lunch time. At dinner time...well you get the picture. Why do I think of compounded daily interest at a time like this?

Dividing the Pie

In the days of Julius Caesar thirteen days were required to send a message from London to Rome. 1900 years later in 1850 it took thirteen days to get a message from London to Rome. In 2005 a message travels from London to Rome in a nano-second. I don't know if the word travel even applies and I can't comprehend how short a nano-second is. Welcome to the information age. Books are cheap and plentiful, the big screen has invaded the home, and research on any subject is beckoned into the home through the Internet. Seminars, schools, self-help programs and associations of all kinds vie for our time and money. Therapists, lawyers and doctors are busy. Our children must be educated to compete in this modern world we say but with all the mountains of information how do we chose the vital information that our short lives and short bank accounts permit?

There are two sections of the Internet that are equal in size and far larger than any other section, pornography and genealogy. One stresses the importance of the stabilizing affect of families in society even from one generation to the next; the other entices instant gratification to the destruction of the family.

What is the one constant that endures through all time and in all circumstances? Human nature. May I suggest an experiment for young mothers? Put your three young preschool children in the back seat of the car and give the one sitting in the middle an ice-cream cone and tell her that it is to be shared among them. Watch closely but secretly (in the mirror) and you will learn the lessons of a socialist democracy. If I don't mention it I'm sure some mother will come up afterward and tell me about the lessons of anarchy.

Tell your two teenagers that there is a piece of their favorite pie and they may share it but tell them that one may cut and the other may choose the piece he wants and you will learn the lessons of separation of power and checks and balances.

We have mentioned the toddlers and the youth so now let's mention the adults. Have your lawyer friend tell his experiences of the old man with money who doesn't leave a will or the old widow with only the rocking chair that has been in the family for generations. Does human nature change from toddler to old age? Can human nature be changed? It can. How? Education, discipline, and persistence, fill the mind with examples out of the best books, study the lives of the great men of history, and study the revelations from God. Once this is done the parent is prepared to teach the child.

Front Porch Repair

Don liked to sit out on his front porch after breakfast before the hot summer day began. He had gotten up at five in time to milk the cows, feed the calves and pigs. The milk truck that picked up his milk cans came by and took his day's production to the cheese plant forty miles away. Often Chuck his cousin would come and sit with him.

Chuck also was a farmer but didn't have any milk cows. However in the summer it wasn't unusual for Chuck to be up at four to bale the hay while the dew was still on it.

They didn't visit much but then one would make a funny remark and then they would laugh. In between laughs the silence stretched out, but it was comfortable.

Generally thirty minutes was enough to let their breakfast settle then they would sigh and go back to work. This particular day however Rusty, a neighbor about their same age came by and he had a problem.

"My baler is broken," he announced.

"What's wrong with it?" Chuck asked.

"Well, you know that big square thing…?" and Rusty held his hands up in a big square.

"There is more than one big square thing," Don pointed out.

"It's the big square thing that the thing jams the hay through." Rusty explained.

"O.K. We are with you." Chuck encouraged. "What about it?"

"Right behind the big square thing is a thing that catches the string and ties it in a knot."

"Oh, the knotter isn't working," Chuck guessed.

"It's working fine," Rusty said. "But right below that thing is a long thing that goes beneath all those things and sticks out the sides. Hooked onto this long thing on each end are two long curved things…"

"That would be the needles," Chuck deduced.

"Yes. The string that comes through a little round thing before it gets to the long curved thing is slack making the string ball up on the thing that ties the bales."

"Right. Trace the string back a little further and you will find the eyelet where the string comes through. Trace back further and you will find a little bracket that is the tensioner. Adjust that until the tension is equal on each string and I think the knotter will do its job. If the tensioner is worn, you can't adjust it, but in that case just take it down to Ed at the Mobile Station and he will fix it for you."

Rusty thanked them for their help and got in his pickup and left.

No sooner was he out of sight than Chuck said, "It would have saved a lot of hassle if Adam had just named everything a thing."

"Yes, you could have just said here comes the big gray thing with the squiggly nose and everyone would think of an elephant," Don hypothesized.

"You would have to say "big gray thing with the squiggly thing growing out his face," Chuck chuckled.

"Growing out his thing," Don refined further.

"There are things to make us live," Chuck intoned.

"And things to make us die."

"Things to build up…"

"And things to break down…."

"Things to make us laugh…"

"And things to make us cry…"

"Things with which to plant…"

"Things that cause birth…"

"And things that cause marriage…"

"Things that cause joy…"

"And things that cause sorrow…"

"Things that cast away stones…"

"And things that gather stones together…"

"Things that rend…"

"And things that sew…"

"Things to love…"

"And things to hate…"

"There are things for every purpose under heaven!"

"Amen, brother. Did we leave any-thing out?"

"The things the banker will take away if I don't go to work." So saying Don got to his feet.

"Things have taken over our lives," Chuck agreed.

The friends and cousins went their own way chuckling of the great philosophy of things.

Feminism 2

I debated whether or not to entitle this essay "Why Women Should not Teach School" but I decided that the subject is much broader than that so I will have two essays called "Feminism" but I still think that women should not teach school. My mother was a school teacher and she confused me so bad. She told me how important education was and she sent me to school every day for twelve years without fail. Then she would turn right around and shake her finger under my nose and tell me,

"Don't get smart!"

My wife says at least I was obedient. Of course my wife was a school teacher also. One day out of the blue and for no reason at all she told me that there is a difference between a wise man and a wise guy and when I said "What's that?" she said, "A wise man doesn't have a smart mouth!" Talk about confusing.

A couple of weeks ago she brought up the subject of the proper role of men and women. It makes me nervous when she wants to talk things over. She says that it's my job to earn and hers to spend, she cooks and I eat. Then she pointed out how much more efficient she is in her job than I am in mine. She says that she can spend more than I can earn and that she can cook more than I can eat.

Some people think that because I am quiet and mild mannered and my wife likes to manage things, that she is the boss but I put her in her place every now and again. Why, just the other day when she came by and said, "You have to get down on your knees if you are going to scrub that floor clean." I told her, "You just move on, woman. I'm mopping this flood and I'll do it any way I want." I'm no wimp, I do the dishes any way I want to and the same with the dusting and making the beds. No woman is going to run me around.

My daughter Rachel comes up with the strangest notions. I lost my job recently and she has two jobs and one pays more per hour than I was making. I pointed this out to her and suggested that we discuss rent. She said, "The law says you have to support me as long as I'm a minor and the second I'm an adult, I'm outta here." When did she become so aware of what the law says? This is the child who was barely old enough to talk, who came leading her brother who was barely old enough to walk, into the house by a flaxen cord around his neck and boasted, "I've taught him to be a husband!"

A few years later, but when she was still small, she declared to the older children when they didn't jump to obey me when I asked them to do something, "Dad's the boss when mom's not home." It makes me wonder what she sees in the home of her friends. This feminist thing, in my opinion has really gotten out of hand. Makes me think maybe I should have kept her home more where she could see how real men and women behave.

But unlike my other daughter she understands about privacy. Her older sibling who was then the baby of the family at the time came into the bath room where I was trying to taking a bath. The wife was already in there to get a hair brush for my oldest daughter who was still little and my oldest son had come in to tinkle. The little one banged the door shut behind her and commanded, "Shut the door and give Dad some privacy!"

Like I said, Tink, that's Rachel's nick name, understands privacy. On her bedroom door hangs the sign under the skull and cross bones, "PRIVATE," "NO TRESPASSING," "VIOLATORS WILL BE PROSECUTED!" On the bottom of the poster is a pile of bones in disarray.

Some things just don't make sense. The women in my life are always telling me that there are going to be more women in heaven than men because those wicked men are always looking at pictures of naked girls and running around with wild women. This is another reason that women should not be allowed to teach school - at least not math! My wife does say I have one thing going for me. She says that if my memory continues to fade I can get into heaven with a clear conscience.

Special Days

Every body has those special days in their lives. For some it is a favorite holiday, for others it's the more personal milestones in one's life, like anniversaries or birthdays. My favorite day is Thanksgiving. Besides being a very grateful person I enjoy the fact that I don't have to buy a present, attend a parade, send cards or go out somewhere to eat. Neither chocolates nor flowers are traditional on this day in our family or in our part of the country. It is a day to spend home with the family which sometimes includes extended family from both sides. I'm never asked to cook so I just spend the day anticipating the feast, feasting the feast and digesting the feast. Sometimes this last activity is done while napping. (My wife just informed me that napping can't be classified as an activity) The ladies do the dishes. What a wonderful day!

Being rather shy during my younger years and not having much experience with the opposite sex it fell to my wife to propose. We were not teenagers by any means. I was working well into my twenty eighth year and had not shown any inclination to rush to the alter. Once in a while I mention the fact that my wife proposed to me and friends look to the wife for verification. She puts this little Mona Lisa smile on her face but says nothing and everybody thinks I'm a liar.

We started our married life in an old service station that had been converted into a home that had been occupied by other small but growing families but it still looked like a service station that had been converted into a home. I remodeled the kitchen and it was quite attractive, then I started on the bath room. We had bought all the plumbing and fixtures but when it was time to install the vanity we were out of money. It seems as if I'm as shy about earning money as I was about kissing the girls. Any way there was plenty of wood in an old horse corral out back so I pulled some of the planks off and built the vanity. I'm quite creative that way. The wife encouraged me with little comment like,

"Well, it looks plenty sturdy." And "I really like the rustic look; it's so in style these days. Did you know that they actually beat new furniture with a chain to make it look old?"

Her parents were a little less certain that I was taking care of their daughter in the manner that she deserved but slowly we began to make a little financial progress and they became hopeful. We were having a good time at one of those Thanksgiving family gatherings. The women, including my mother-in-law, were in the kitchen getting dinner ready to put on the table. My father-in-law was standing in a doorway visiting with them while they worked. I was down the hall in the east room entertaining the nieces and nephews when the wife dropped a huge glass bowl filled with pink jello that shattered with a huge pop. The wife screamed with horror because she had just ruined one of the traditional Thanksgiving dishes.

I, of course not having seen what had happened, thought that some real disaster had occurred so I leapt to my feet and went racing down the hall into the kitchen. The instant the wife saw me she threw her arms protectively above her head and pled, "Don't beat me! Don't beat me!"

She thought that was pretty funny but her parents…Let me just say that ten years later while at another family gathering when I said to the wife "Would you like to go down to the field with me and hold the flashlight while I change the water?" and she answered and said, "This isn't our anniversary date is it?" her folks exchanged knowing glances.

After another ten years the wife was telling her family on the phone about how she and the children went up into the hills to cut a Christmas tree and got stuck in the mud. After walking for an hour it got dark and cold and they had to stop and make a fire to thaw out their frozen wet feet. It was quite an adventure. They saw an elk only a few rods away and she told about how beautiful the stars were that night. No, she had not been a bit worried for the family knew where they had gone and she was confident that a rescue party would soon be out and they were. My oldest son and my son-in-law showed up and pulled the truck out of the mud and followed them home to make sure they got home safe.

"Where was Dave?" They asked.

"Oh, he was home lying on the front room couch," the wife informed them.

I didn't even bother to get on the other phone and clarify that I had a sprained ankle that was black clear to the knee and throbbed terribly if I lowered it below the level of my heart and was so swollen I couldn't even get my toe in a shoe.

Video Camera

Memo: From Dave\ Manager Fillmore Dock
To: Truck Video Camera Supervisor

I'm well aware that the company does not acknowledge that there are Video cameras in the trucks; nevertheless I deem it my duty, for safety and personal comfort reasons, to point out personal experiences that I'm sure I have in common with other drivers.

One morning as I was exiting I -15 at Scipio my cell phone buzzed just as I was pulling through the stop sign. Just at that moment I had my breakfast sandwich in one hand and the other hand was busy with the steering wheel. Also I had to shift up to beat the traffic. The sandwich hand I then had to steer with and the other hand then was busy with the gear shift.

How was I to answer the phone? With my natural resourcefulness I quickly kicked off one boot and with a lighting quick shuffle my hand went from gear shift to pocket (containing phone) to foot and back to gear shift. Now holding the phone to my ear with my foot I was ready to answer. Have you ever tried to swallow a big hunk of cheese that hasn't been chewed well enough? Quickly grasping the seriousness of the situation, I threw myself forward executing a perfect Heimlich maneuver on myself on the steering wheel. I'll probably have to have a hip replacement when I'm older.

Now I was faced with an opaque windshield, (bits of cheese and bread liberally sprayed with great force) I've missed a gear and stalled in the intersection. Horns began honking, followed by hand gestures and aspersions cast upon my noble ancestry. Despite all these challenges I was able to answer the phone. It was Jami. "Dave, I have a pickup for you and the directions are quite complicated. Do you have a paper and pencil ready?"

I'm almost certain I heard someone laughing before I hung up.

Now, just let me say that although I think Jami is a very intelligent, responsible, pleasant, lovely, and talented young lady, I think someone with less youthful exuberance and mischief should monitor the truck video cameras, perhaps an older, and more sedate and serious person.

Sincerely,
D. L. Hatton

Can't even scratch..........or pick your nose............Heaven forbid I should sing........ Wish the radio worked............Gotta learn to make the cell phone chime rather than vibrate..........talk about tickle…….

Family Tree

Andy is a lovely woman. She is trim and shapely, has nice facial features and her expression is cheerful and pleasant. Her dark hair, now liberally laced with white, is always nicely groomed and I must say it is always a pleasure to see her. She is married to my wife's uncle and they live in a distant town so we seldom see her. It is only natural as we get older to not be able to keep track of all the nieces and nephews and the grand-nieces and nephews are sometimes almost strangers. The occasion for the family gathering escapes me for the moment but the whole large family was there from infants in arms to the older ones getting around by leaning on a cane. It was no surprise then that Andy upon arrival thought that Eve our oldest was Dana's daughter. Now Dana is my wife's sister and has a daughter named Tana who has the same colorings as our daughter and is about the same age and they have been mistaken one for another all their lives.

Natural mistake, but then Eve who is unmarried was holding Jessie's, my other daughter's, baby and standing next to her husband, Jon. Now Jessie looks a lot like Terena who is Dana's oldest daughter and when she came to get her baby Andy thought she was Terena. But just then Terena came and wanted to hold the baby and said, "Come to momma you pretty baby."

Now Andy still thought Eve was married to Jon but she couldn't decide who the baby belonged to. Jon said it was his so then Andy thought that maybe Jon wasn't married to Eve but to Terena my daughter and the baby was theirs. About that time Kurt, Terena's husband came and affectionately put his arm around his wife Terena and looking down at the baby said, "How is our baby doing?"

Poor Andy by this time was totally confused. Jessie, my daughter then clarified that she was married to Jon. Now it was clear that Jon was not my son-in-law and Jessie was not my daughter but that Terena was my daughter and Kurt my son-in law. It had to be this way because she had just been told that the baby was my granddaughter.

They tried again. Finally it got straighten out that Jon and Jessie were the parents of the baby and that Jessie was my daughter. By that time Tana, Dana's daughter had joined the group and wanted to hold the baby and she said, "Come to Aunt Tana." Now Tana, silly goose is not the baby's aunt but a second cousin, or some such relation. (I think I'm getting confused) Anyway, now Andy thought that Tana was my daughter but then who was Eve? Andy of course came to the conclusion that Eve was Dana's daughter. You have to admit that you couldn't fault Andy's logic.

The party must have been a success for the huge meal got consumed and the buzz of visiting voices was constant. The kids ran up and down the large hall with their cousins, favorite family stories were told, but finally people started to leave. By this time two of my wife's other aunts had rehearsed Andy until she knew who my wife's children were and who belonged to her sister Dana.

On our way out, my wife and I stopped to say goodbye to her three aunts who were visiting together.

"Your daughter Eve is such a wonderful little gal." Andy said to me. "She is so fun to talk to."

"Eve's not mine." I contradicted, "She belongs to Dana."

Poor Andy's face fell and her shoulders slumped. She put her hand over her eyes. It had taken a full two hours to get the family tree straight and she had just learned it all wrong. When the two other aunts started beating me Andy realized that she had been had and joined enthusiastically in the fray. The funny thing is that I had not heard nor known of the struggle that Andy had gone through to get the families straight. I don't know why I said that. I learned from Eve later on about the whole confusion episode. Of course nobody believes in my innocence. And even if I were innocent this time, they say, I would have said the exact same thing if I had known so I'm just as guilty. What kind of justice system is that?

The Philosophy of Dating

I've come up with an idea that is going to make me one of the wealthiest men on the face of the earth. I'm going to write a dictionary that will be bought by every mature male person on the face of the earth. To begin with it will come out in English but then will be expanded to include all languages and people. This first dictionary will be a Femineeze to English translation. I've overcome all the challenges and obstacles but one…I can't find an interpreter. In the mean time men will have to depend upon the empirical method of dealing with women.

Now, it will be very apparent that I was born in the first half of the last century and that my view of dating is very antiquated. In those days the guy asked the girl out several days in advance after having made arrangements with dad to take the family car. He would dress in nice slacks and shirt and she in a dress or skirt with high heels and nylons. Whether it was dance or movie, dinner was part of the evening. The guy would pick the girl up at home where he was obliged to sit for a few minutes and visit the family. During these short visits the dad had a chance to assess him and the little sisters to fall in love with him or not but they would always voice their opinion in the most forthright manner once he was gone. Porch lights were left on and dad waited up until she was home, safe and inside.

Sounds pretty boring I know but the kids knew how to have fun. Not that I ever joined in the ritual for I lacked several things, dad, car and girlfriend but don't think that I didn't know what was going on; I was the designated driver. This means I was the one without a date. Alright! There was another type of designated driver but the girls in my high school didn't drink so it was the same as today…in this one respect but in others it was different. The designated driver was the one that could pile the other boys in a heap in the back seat and then keep the car between the lines until they were all home safe. Did I mention I was usually the designated driver in these situations also?

The system wasn't perfect but the guy was still responsible for the girl to the parents. Those that couldn't control themselves quickly became man and wife.

Nowadays it's all different. The young people don't date they just hang out. I've asked my children what that means precisely but they can't define it, however I think I have it figured out. On rare occasions I have driven by groups just hanging out. The girls do it by wearing low rider jeans and short blouses that leave about six inches to hang out. The guys do it by wearing their jeans so low that their fannies "hang out". When the guys and girls stand around together like this it's called hanging out together.

Of course it is hard for parents to know who the girl is hanging out with but even if they did all youth are considered hangers in common. There are no boyfriend-girl friend combos they just glide from one partner to another. I've heard of hang gliders but all the different versions have me confused. Some say that if the currents are just right one can stay up for hours but this probably only refers to the druggies that hang together. Jargon that describes this type of hanging is soaring or sailing. It's probably some kind of code or language that I'm unfamiliar with but I plan to research this further.

Co-habitation is also described as hanging out together just as the group down at the parking lot. I guess the same expression has different degrees sort of like Masonry but the nuances are a little too fine for me yet. This has replaced courtship. Courtship, way back when, was a serious endeavor to get to know a person with whom one was contemplating marriage. The couple spent a lot of time together and of course they tried to be on their best behavior. If the courtship covered a long spell the prospective mate either learned self control trying to impress the suitor or had time to display his temper or other character flaws. Now days they "let it all hang out" right from the first day they move in together. This is both a physical and psychological thing.

If the first try doesn't work it is back home to daddy then back to the parking lot then to another apartment. Daddy, parking lot, apartment; this cycle is known as the Bermuda triangle where many mysterious navel disasters have taken place but still draws the curious and unwary.

I must now talk about the dangerous transition from dating and courting to hanging out. This began during the time in history in my area when I was between high school age and marriage. This period naturally was much longer for me than for most in my era so I got to suffer through the whole course.

Gifts

It does take but a few years of marriage for a man to figure out that it is wise to ask the wife well in advance what she would like for Christmas. This way he will have plenty of time to save the money and to purchase the gift. Besides that, he will know exactly where to find it on December 24th when he stops by on his way home from work. This will also give her time to forget what she asked for so she will act surprised…this also might have something to do with the fact that the store where he has stopped on his way home from work on December 24th has just sold the last one and he is forced to buy something else.

I remember the year that I placed an order for her present in August. It's true I swear it. But of course the best laid plans can come to naught. I don't remember what I bought her on the way home from work on December 24th but I do remember that the thing I had ordered didn't come until August. She was thrilled with it and hugged and kissed me. I smiled and wished her happy birthday. Her birthday is in September. For a day she showed off her new gift but then right in the middle of showing it to a visitor she stopped. "Wait a minute! This was my Christmas present for last year! What are you trying to pull?" It was worth a try and because I distinctly remember buying her a Christmas present on the way home from work on December 24th. I figured I was one ahead; didn't work.

One year I forgot to buy her a birthday present. In my defense I pointed out that we had been married for thirty years and we had been nearly the same age at the time of the aforementioned marriage but now she was years younger and because I had bought many more presents than she had had birthdays I must be considered a very generous and loving husband willing to go the extra mile. Mathematical logic is not the way to convince a wife, I can assure you. They are right brain creatures...always right!

One year I bought her a new deer rifle. I had wanted one for years but since I didn't have the money for two I sacrificed and gave the beautiful thing to her. She really enjoyed shooting it and she let me take it hunting the next year. She really is quite generous in some ways but no more generous than I. The sewing machine she bought me that year I let her use continually. In fact I've never sewn a stitch on it.

The year she gave me a wheat grinder I bought her a waffle iron. Our daughter got a toaster that year from some anonymous person. Desiree, our neighbor shook her head and said that we had been married too long.

This year the wife is getting a new floor in the east room that is to be my new office. She gave me the second hand desk her friend gave to her because it was too big for her office upstairs. It is made of very beautiful old wood I discovered after I took off two coats of paint and one of varnish and sanded it down. I could even get the drawers open after I repaired the automatic lock.

Another memorable Christmas on my way home from work on December 24th, I stopped at the lumber yard. While I waited for some help the neighbor lady, Frankie came in.

"What are you doing here, Dave?"

"I'm buying my wife a Christmas present," I said.

"What are you getting for her?"

"Some two by fours," I answered.

She looked at me a little askance so I added,

"I know…when the women in Kanosh hear of this they will be glad they are not married to me at Christmas time."

"Dave, the women in Kanosh are glad all year long they are not married to you!"

Although my son lives a hundred and fifty miles to the south he drove up to a town sixty miles to the east of where I live to pick up the parcels that he delivered each day. Because I was substituting for a friend I had to be in the same town to deliver out of a small semi I drove. I found out that the first costumer I was to deliver to was not open for business till eight so I drove over to say hello to my son and to wish him happy birthday. After the first hellos and a happy birthday wish I asked him if I had bought him a present that year. He said that I had. I then asked him if I had been generous. He again said that I had, quite generous in fact. Before I could ask him what I had bought for him his freight showed up and he had to get to work. I forgot about it for some time and by the time I remembered to ask him and his mother what I had bought for him they had forgotten. To this day I don't know what I bought him for his birthday but I guess the important thing is that I was generous.

Sorry to cut this essay on gift giving short but I've got to get down town before the stores close and of course they will be closed tomorrow. It's a holiday, ya know.

In the Mood

My wife has always liked plaques to stick on the wall or refrigerator. The kitchen is her favorite place for these but there have always been some in the office and the living room also. One of her favorites that she had over the kitchen sink for a number of years said; "Kitchen closed, Not in the mood." It was a cute little sign and it garnered some laughs occasionally from friends and family over the years. The wife was pretty good at taking care of meal time but there were times that I think the sign had its affect on her. One day she came home with a new plaque that she like so much she framed it behind glass and hung it in the family room. It said, "There is no more beautiful picture than that of a good woman cooking a meal for those she loves."

After we had gone through a little period of time when the plaque in the kitchen seemed to be on the ascendancy, I, while the wife was gone, got the plaque from the family room and hung it on the wall next to the "Not in the mood" plaque and then I waited to see what would happen. I was a little disappointed when the wife never said a word but a couple of days later the "Not in the mood" plaque disappeared.

Some weeks later I learned that the plaque had not been given to the thrift store like I had assumed but had merely gone into storage, "just in case". I've never summoned up the courage to ask "In case of what?" My intuition tells me this is one of those times I should wait to ask when she is in the right mood.

Of course every husband knows he doesn't need a plaque in the bedroom to tell him the mood. If the lights are turned down low it means that she is in the mood to sleep and doesn't want you stumbling over things in the dark and waking her up when you come to bed. If the lights are all ablaze that means she is in the mood to read. If there is nothing but an incense candle burning that means that the power is off.

There are things that husbands can do to enhance a mood and if done at just the right time are quite effective. For instance, the mood called "gritas emotionales"* can be induced by entering the kitchen just as the wife is scraping the toast and declaring "I thought I heard you calling me for breakfast."

A husband's rate of success is quite high in these areas but rather low in others. "Your song" is playing on the radio and you hold out your arms and say "They are playing our song. Wanna dance?" She gives you that level stare out from under her hat and declines by pointing out there are several hundred bales of hay left to haul. You can see them plainly from the back of the flatbed. At this point your teenage daughter abruptly lets out on the clutch and jerks your legs out from under you and*

---

* Emotional yelling

the mood is gone. Well, actually it is not gone but it is changed; there is now more mood.

We discussed repainting and decorating the living room but she declared she was in a blue mood and couldn't focus on the project. She said for me to just go ahead and decorate it any way I wanted. Several days later as I took the lid off a can of sky blue paint she looks over my shoulder and says, "You're not going to paint the room that color are you?"

"Yeah, why not?"

"Blue is a cold color and will always put me in a blue mood. Yellow is a warm, comfortable color."

"The color of the curtains doesn't match the walls," she opines a few days later.

"The curtains match the walls now but clash with the furniture."

"When you plan to redecorate a room you should consider the color of the flooring. The right flooring really finishes off the whole scheme and blends everything else together."

Several other helpful little hints concerning picture frames and wall hangings were invaluable but finally the day came when we had our first party to show off our new room. My wife got lots of complements on it but very graciously said,

"My husband did the whole thing."

Our neighbor, Cynthia thought that I should go into the home decorating business but somehow

I lacked the confidence to work on other peoples' homes.

Carpentry

To give my boys experience and to teach them how to work I decided that I would build the shop that I had always needed and wanted. I had been gathering materials for years and finally had enough to get the building up and roofed against the storms. I could finish the rest as time and money permitted. Part of my accumulated materials were several windows given to me by a neighbor. These windows were of various sizes and shapes but I figured that one type I could put on the ends of the building and another on the back. A large sliding glass door laid on its side would serve as the big front window.

There were to be four long narrow windows across the back that were tinted because they had come from a green house but still they would admit plenty of light. The two windows on the east end of the shop slipped right into place and I secured them with the wife's help. Pleased that they fit so well I casually commented on my skills.

However the two windows on the west, much to my chagrin, were an inch longer and I had to reframe the wall to get them to fit. I casually mentioned to my wife about how one would assume that windows all from the same place that looked identical would be the same size and if they had been they would have fit perfectly too.

"I can see that they would have," she agreed but she had that little smirk on her face. That look really annoys me and she knows it. Some two days later a friend came to visit while the boys and I were working on the shop again. My friend Roland helped me carry the big glass door from the shed in the back of the lot up to shop. The thing was heavy and we set it down inside near where it was to be placed in the wall while we caught our breath. Not being able to stand to have something interesting going on without her, the wife, while we were still resting came out to the shop. I saw her coming and put on a big, long face.

"What's the matter?" she said the minute she entered.

"I've got to reframe that wall. The window is too big for the opening," I groaned.

"Really?" she commiserated; she tries hard not to smirk in front of company. But then she remembers that it is against my nature to admit I've screwed up especially in front of friends and her eyes narrow. "Are you sure?"

"Hold the tape." I tell her and indicate she put it on the edge of the gap for the window. "92 inches, see there?" she reads the tape which verifies my declaration.

"Now hold the tape on the end of the window." She complies.

"96 inches." I declare and show her the measurement. She has read the tape both times and there is no room for argument. I slump back down on the saw horse and sigh.

"Well, I guess you better get busy then." It's harder for her not to smirk this time but she managed well by turning her back and heading for the door.

Just before she disappears I exclaim.

"Wait a minute! I've got an idea. Hold that tape up again Roland. Look, this metal frame around the window is just four inches! If we remove it, and it would be easy just these four screws hold it in place, it would fit perfectly!"

"Damned, you!" The wife makes a disgusted noise in her throat and whisked out the door. The guys all laugh. We remove the metal frame and slip the window in place. It fits perfectly. We chuckle again.

"That was rather entertaining, don't you think?" I couldn't help but brag on my accomplishment.

"It was," my sons admitted.

"It's gonna cost you!" Roland grinned.

"Yes, but it was so satisfying," I said.

It cost me!

Love and Marriage

Over the last forty years as I have been contemplating, then practicing marriage I have had many opportunities to discuss the subject, especially in the rapidly changes mores of society. When I was young, people graduated from high school, began college or universities studies, got married, raised a family and the cycle was expected to go round and round in the season thereof but now with the new, anything goes life styles, love and marriage seem to be two independent players. Gay marriages, partnerships, mixed marriages (has a different connotation than race and religion), open marriages and universal marriages are terms now being discussed. Polygamy and polyandry must be given a second look in our anything goes world. We are told that we are on the cutting edge of societal evolution. Not quite.

Biblical history early on speaks of polygamy and explains under what circumstances it was to be practiced. It was not done away with officially among the Jews until the year 1020 although it had fallen into disuse because of the economic difficulty it imposes on a people in exile. The Muslims practice it to this day. Polyandry was practiced by the Eskimos for who knows how long. Biblical history also speaks of cities of gays in the days of

Abraham and again centuries later in a city among the Benjamites.

The people of the tribe of Benjamin were almost destroyed and the survivors were left without women. They were given permission by the other tribes to steal wives from Judah. Some of these people were not happy so they migrated north and established a little colony that became know as Sparta.

Plato describes very well the curious mixture of marriages and planned parenthood of Sparta reminiscent of our day. In other words there is nothing new under heaven. Cato, the Roman statesman, describes the feminist movement of his day and asserts that the woman didn't seek to be equal but superior.

The extreme feminists of our day declare that all men have the Hebrew point of view and are all polygamists at heart and that all intimate relations between man and woman are a form of rape. A woman is only totally fulfilled when she has had a lesbian experience.

The male chauvinists declare that women have the Greek point of view and want independence, power and money and sex only when they are in the mood.

During a discussion on the above topics by a group of friends here at home my wife asked me,

"Aren't men all polygamists at heart?"

"Well, yes, but they have to be just to survive even in a monogamous society."

The wife got a little smirk on her face. She loves to be right. She pursed it further.

"How so?"

"A man has to be able to love three women."

"His mother, his wife and his daughter?" was the guess.

"No, he has to love the little sweetheart he married, the changeling he finds in his bed one morning that looks just like the little sweetheart but says things like 'I'm pregnant and the thought of kissing you makes me want to throw up,' and the stranger that replaces the changeling who says 'I'm having a hot flash and I'm exercising every bit of self control I have to keep my self from murdering you. Why don't you go out and work in your shop today.'?"

I got a good laugh with that one. I spent an extra day in the shop.

One day a good friend and his wife who live in a distant town came to visit me. During the course of the conversation he asked me, "If you lost your wife do you think that you would remarry?"

"I might under the right circumstances."

"What are the right circumstances?"

"She would have to be a woman with an honest heart, highly intelligent, healthy, young, beautiful, rich, and madly in love with me."

The friend looked at me a moment and said,

"You are perfectly safe then."

"I am," I acknowledged and we laughed.

Sitting in a discussion at school (I went back to school in my old age) with the class that consisted of two or three older students and many young ones, we got on the subject of feminism, love, marriage, and related subjects. It was pointed out that Isaiah prophesied that in the last days the women would rule over them and children would be their oppressors. Of course the ruled over were the men. Many disastrous things were to be the result of such an arrangement but the end result was that the wicked women and most of the men were to be killed in the wars leaving seven women to one man.

One of the older female students made the comment that the men would love that especially because the women would provide their own living suggesting that the polygamous nature of man is more carnal than otherwise. The younger men admitted that would be factor to induce the man to accept such an arrangement. The women tended to believe that men were essentially selfish in this and just didn't want to learn to practice self control. On certain cycles of the month and at times when a woman was not in the mood the husband could just walk on down the hall to another wife.

None of the women suggested however that the woman exercise self control and get in the mood and be thoughtful of the husband. As the discussion was winding down and I had not said a word I was finally asked if I hoped that I would still be alive when the time came to take seven wives.

"Heaven forbid!" I cried.

Much to my surprise the women didn't like my answer. It didn't make sense I thought at first but then the reason came to me. Although the women didn't like polygamy they did like the fact that men liked woman so much they wanted a lot of them. In denying that I wanted more than one wife I denied also the possibility that women were so great that two were better than one and maybe they even interpreted my answer to mean that even one was not all that great and the not so great wife would be as good as any other woman and that the increase in number would not be an increase in pleasure for me. I was not popular that day. Well, that day especially.

The conclusion of the discussion that day was that men liked the Hebrew world view of woman because of the increased carnal pleasure that included the expansion of the ego. The more wives the richer and better and more honored he became. He chose this view for essential selfish reasons.

The women liked the Greek world view because it gave to women the independence, income, honor and self esteem they deserved. The woman then had control of her life to pick her partner among many like the men under their polygamous system. If a child was wanted she could pick the sperm donor. She could have her pleasures when ever the mood struck her.

The feminist movement has focused on the differences between men and women and has promoted an adversarial climate but in the final analysis men are not from Mars and women are not from Venus. The failures of communication are not because of the differences but because humans, all of us, men and women, are so much alike. It has been said that divorce is caused by selfishness. I believe this to be true. Sometimes it is the selfishness of one person but often it is the selfishness of two. All of the alternate life styles and alternate marriages are based on self gratification and carry selfishness to another level. Sometimes it is openly admitted but in general it is not.

Love and marriage don't always go together but love in marriage happens more frequently than love without marriage. One more piece of advice; men if you possibly can, buy a large lot in the country side and built a nice house for the wife on one corner and a shop on the other, at least thirty yards away but fifty is better.

Law Enfarcement

My wife likes to do crafts and has her little projects all over the house. We can't go on a trip without her taking along her knitting or crocheting. When she complains that I don't take her anywhere I think "Why spend all that money driving around the country when you don't look at anything but your work? You never see anything." I even thought of buying a vibrator chair for her to sit in and just telling her we are on a trip. It would be much cheaper in the long run. You notice I tell you of my thoughts. Over the years I've learned to keep them to myself.

When a friend of mine offered me a large old loom that was missing a few parts and pieces I promptly declined. Where would we put such a thing? I didn't know anything about looms. Who would repair it and refinish it? My friend then informed me that he had already talked with my wife and she was very enthusiastic about it but he said that she said that he had best talk to me before bringing it over... The family room was now the loom room. Hours and hours of hard work later I had the wood of the newly repaired loom gleaming. Of course now she informed me that she needed the accessories. Everyone knows that when a woman gets something new there are always accessories.

First I built her a bench to sit on while she wove, several kinds of shuttles, a slaying hook and several other things that might be unique to our loom. Soon she had a little business going selling pioneer rugs. A friend of ours saw the weaving operation and thought that it would be great for her students down at the elementary school where she taught to see how things were made in the old days. Since this friend lived on the other end of the state I had to take the loom apart and load it on the pickup. Finally everything was ready and the wife left but as she started up the ramp to get on the freeway she thought that she had better experiment with the steering on the truck because I had just had the front end rebuilt and driving it now was different. About ten seconds into the experiment the highway patrol pulled her over. He thought that she was drunk.

Luckily he was a good friend of ours and he knew the wife didn't drink. He asked what the big contraption in the back was and she told him it was a loom. My wife blames me for starting the rumor that the cop pulled her over for weaving down the road. She says my sense of humor is warped.

Not long after my oldest daughter got her driver's license she backed into the gate that leads down the lane to our back lot. She was in the huge old utility van that we had converted into a passenger van because the family had grown so. The van wasn't hurt and my daughter spent a couple of hours helping me repair the gate. All things considered it was a good and inexpensive lesson for her and of course she got teased by her siblings.

"Look out!" they would holler one to another, "she's backing out now!"

Years later after my daughter had struck out on her own two or three times she had come home for the summer and was driving the same old van. Carefully she looked up and down the street before backing out of the driveway but no sooner had she backed around into her lane she heard the crunch and felt the jar. She had backed into the deputy sheriff. The Sheriff sat in the passenger's seat. They had been backing out of the driveway from the other side of the street. Both these men were boyhood friends. I went out to see what was going to transpire. The Sheriff said that he couldn't investigate an accident that he had been involved in so they called the Highway Patrol. The patrolman that showed up was the same friend that had pulled the wife over for weaving down the road. My wife had been in the kitchen dicing potatoes while all of this was transpiring but now she came out to see what was going on. She got right into the investigation and of course was making sure that her little girl was dealt with fairly. She was excited but not mad or unreasonable or anything like that but she was emphasizing her points with abrupt gestures. Finally the patrolman decided that the two drivers were equally responsible for the accident and that he would issue no citation.

"That is the only right decision and I commend you for your fairness!" The wife said with a sharp chopping gesture toward the patrolman's chest.

"His decision might have had more to do with your threatening him with a butcher knife," I observed. The wife had forgotten all about the knife in her excitement but the patrolman had kept a close eye on it as the wife waved it under his nose and jabbed it at his belly to emphasis her arguments. The wife was absolutely mortified to find the knife in her hand. She blushed, she hide it behind her back while we all laughed at her.

Several days later as I was making my rounds on the delivery truck I stopped at the auto repair shop to deliver body parts and there sat the deputy's pickup truck with the crumpled fender.

"What is it going to cost to fix this?" I asked.

"One thousand dollars," came the reply.

Once again the daughter got off easy. The old van suffered a cracked taillight lens and dent that looked like it might have made by a golf ball.

Not long after that I ran into the patrolman.

"You know my wife don't you?" he said to me.

"I do. She must be the troll that sits under the bridge and threatens the Billy Goats Gruff."

"Pardon me?"

"She is married to you and you are the Highway Pa Troll."

Back to School

I got truckers kidney (kidney stone) and my doctor told me that I should find another line of work. She told me this right after she punched me in the kidney and I about fainted with pain and she said that I had the classical symptoms. My wife was there and when she suggested that I go back to school and get a degree I just said, "Sign me up." The next thing I knew I was getting ready to go get a classical liberal education and of course I had the classical freshmen jitters, squared. That's a math term, I'm told. My basic math skills, that I developed in high school tells me that I haven't been in school for……..38 years.

My wife told me to relax, my skills would quickly return once I got into the swing of things but my two greatest areas of achievement aren't even offered and at my age…basketball and beer. You can see that I'm in trouble.

I have to drink a lot of lemon water for my kidney health and of course any pressure on my stomach shortens the time I can sit in class so I bought me some new bibs (bib overalls) because they are so comfortable but they sure cost a lot… inflation, ya know. After the second week in school I told my wife I wasn't sure I should wear my bibs to class. And she said, "Why not?"

"Well, the younger, poorer students can't afford bibs and I don't want them to feel bad."

"Nobody is going to accuse you of being ostentatious," she said.

"I don't care nothing about that...I just don't want them to think I'm showing off.!"

"If it makes you uncomfortable maybe you should wear what the other older men wear."

"They are all kids but the professor."

"What does he wear?"

"White shirts and ties."

"Why don't you try that?" she suggested, but when I went upstairs and changed then she said that ties don't go well with bibs so I went back up stairs and took the tie off. She put her hand over her eyes like she does when she gets a headache. I had her lie down and I put a cool damp cloth on her head. I'm quite considerate that way.

I had a good day in class today. The professor asked if everybody knew what an oxy-moron was. I raised my hand and he called on me.

"We had one of them once," I said. "She came to her grain real good but when you sat down to milk her she would kick you all over the farm. When I said she was the dumbest animal on earth my wife said that sheep were dumber. In fact she said that the term smart sheep was an oxy-moron. Now I know that in the bible it refers to sheep as cattle but an ox is of the bovine species and sheep just don't qualify. Now, I don't want you to think that my wife is dumb. She is a college graduate and does real good in the academic world, but she just don't know nothing about farming."

I had to have an oral exam. This is different than going to the dentist. You sit up in front of the whole class and two professors fire questions at you. Sometimes family members come also and of course my wife wanted to come to see if I was learning anything but she sat in the back and made signs or signals and I was afraid that the professors would think that she was giving me the answers so I had to explain that she was just using body language that I had learned to recognize after having been married to her for so long. We weren't cheating. Hiding her eyes with one hand means "I'm so embarrassed." Putting her hands on the sides of her eyes like blinders on a horse means "I hope nobody sees me." Finger tips over the mouth from below means "He'll never get away with that!" And of course when she sits with her legs crossed and her back turned halfway towards me means "I don't know him!" After I explained the professors seemed to understand and quit watching her. It's hard to go back to school after all these years.

Kant

I would like to give some advice to the new student of Kant. First and foremost, you should memorize Webster's New Collegiate Dictionary. This won't help a bit in understanding Kant but it is easier and perhaps your professor might be impressed by this feat and let you off the hook. If not then you should learn the German language, for Kant was a German philosopher. You still won't understand him but this too will be easier and you might get a degree in languages. If, by this time, you haven't come to your senses then you must study the ancient Chinese dialect of Kantonese.

I think it would be helpful at this point to translate some of the most often used terms from Kantonese into modern English. Intuition in one sense is a foreknowledge not connected with the sensual that he defines as empirical or of the material world discerned by the five senses. He calls this type of intuition a priori. A priori is truth that is self-evident. A priori common to all people, he says, is time and space. However I intuit a third, the light of Christ or conscience, knowledge of right and wrong, equality under the law, sacredness of life, of liberty and property, or more simply put, fairness.

My own empirical intuition (intuition based on the sensual) of manifold unity of consciousness (manifold meaning folding the many into one as does the exhaust manifold in gasoline engines combines from many ports into one the exhaust) is based upon an ever reoccurring phenomenon.

Although a little girl is too young to add or subtract or even count she cries, "Mommy, David has more cookies than I do. That's not fair!"

David on the other hand introduces the transcendental synthesis of imagination by saying;

"But I'm bigger than you and I need more food."

While the little girl is cogitating the synthetical unity of the apperception of the manifold of sensuous intuition David eats the cookies.

Since this worked so well on my little sister ---I mean since this worked so well for David he decided to try this on his wife. The day after Thanksgiving there remained only one piece of pumpkin pie which the wife was preparing to eat.

"You're not going to eat my pie are you?" he asked.

"Your pie? What makes it your pie?"

"Intuition."

She narrowed her eyes.

"Cogitate on justice for just a moment. You do want to be fair don't you?"

"Of course, but since you had more pie than I did yesterday then it is just that I eat this piece today."

"Let's consider the a priori of the transcendental intuitions namely time, space, and fairness."

"Twenty-four hours have gone by and now I have plenty of space for pie."

"Don't get cute. Justice, you say, will be served if you eat the pie but let's consider the manifold apperceptions of the original intuition, namely that of our size, weight and bone structure at the time of our marriage. I, a male in this corner weighing 160 lbs. and six foot high with medium bone structure, and you in that corner being female at 117 lbs. and five foot five with small bone structure. Now mathematics being of transcendental intuition rather than empirical apperceptions leaves no doubt upon the subject since the ratios of our proper body weight and not of actual body weight definitely demonstrates that you have already consumed the ratio of the pie corresponding to that weight.Of course conversely that leaves this last piece of pie to balance the ratios properly by my eating it.

"Don't pull that proper body weight maneuver on me."

"Hey, this isn't just a metaphysical exercise, this is pure reason."

"Phooey, you just want to have the pleasure of eating it instead of me."

"Consider this in light of the new diet program you are following. A healthy body, you tell me is maintained by the proper ph balance, this being the acid and alkaline. And since your body is way too acid you should eat foods that are alkaline. One of the very best ways to alkalinize the body is to eat slowly and chew you food very well. Now since your mouth and teeth are much smaller than mine then the smaller bites you should take would remain in the mouth the same amount of time as would my food if we both chew properly. Hence the empirical or sensual enjoyment would be equal only if I eat this last piece of pie. Empirical and sensual enjoyment in this case is the sense of taste and smell.

Not only that but the transcendental intuition of fairness expressed in Christianity as "Love thy neighbor as thyself" comes into play because I want you to be healthy so that I can continue to enjoy your company. Not only that but your actual body weight demonstrates that for many years your manifold empirical or sensual enjoyments have been superior to mine and have resulted in the phenomenon known commonly as habit. This being the case the transcendental intuition of fairness based in love in its manifold manifestations dictates that I eat the pie."

"Did you just call me fat?" she asked.

This weak attempt to shift my solid reasoning off its base was useless. We both knew that she was completely out classed in this argument. I won.

She ate the pie!

Not only that but she said;

"I intuit that you are not going to get any supper."

I didn't.

I wonder if Kant was married. I wonder if he had to re-Kant much.

My head hurts. I'm going to bed.

Conspiracy

This essay is not for the squeamish, the naive' or the mentally obtuse. Any person of any experience whatsoever will tell you that knowing will save your hide whereas proof must often wait for another day. It is in this light I write which will be evident as the story progresses. I have no time to look out for the unwary, prove to the skeptic, or animate the indolent but the truth will be evident to the alert, the intelligent, the knowing.

As often happens, it began innocently enough. It was just after Christmas and as usual I had over indulged in Christmas cheer of one kind or another and found myself with a little head cold. (I can resist anything but temptation.) I started the normal procedures to handle such things and the cold progressed pretty much like they all do but suddenly it decided to settle in my ear. I stepped up the medication and soon had it under control. I felt it the moment it went into my other ear and knew I was in trouble. Two days later I found myself in the emergency room of the hospital. It was Saturday morning and the clinic where my doctor works is closed for the week end but there is a doctor on call. She is a young lady that is very pregnant. The same doctor who two years before handled my kidney stone.

After asking me my symptoms she punched me in the kidney and when I screamed and was left gasping and with my eyes bugging out she said; Classic case of kidney stones."

Next she had the nurse check my blood pressure which was high she said, "Sometimes pain will make the blood pressure go up."

Anyway here I am with both ears aching lying on the exam table having my blood pressure checked. My ears are completely plugged and I can't hear a thing. The next thing I know the curtain is being pulled around me and my wife is motioning for me to stand up which I do. Now the nurse, the doctor, and the wife all approach and are smiling so sweetly. They are asking me things but I can't hear a thing they are saying but trying to be agreeable and please them I nod and shrug. They all look pleased and happy. Suddenly my wife uncouples the straps on my bib overalls and I have to make a desperate grab to save my dignity. My shorts are pulled down off my behind from behind and I feel the coolness of an alcohol wipe, but before I can react the sting of a needle prick follows and that by a long steady painful injection of serum.

When I got a glimpse of the syringe I could tell it was about the size I used on the five hundred pound heifers back when I was a dairyman. They usually bawled too. By the time I had my clothes picked off the floor and buckled in place the women were on the other side of the room going over the paper work. They were still smiling and chuckling and visiting amongst themselves confident that I couldn't hear but they knew I was no longer in the dark and they didn't venture near. It was no secret that I was sore.

Now, to the amateur this little story I have just told may seem like a plot among three women to get a cantankerous old man to go to the doctor and get his ears fixed but it goes much deeper than that. Who puts drops in my ears for pain that no longer exists; but neither does my hearing. Who can't use the telephone any more? Have you noticed that women are like the word ubiquitous? Nobody knows what it means but it's everywhere. Notice the doctor in this story was a woman. The Senators from California are both women. The Person most likely to be our next president is a woman. Two Supreme Court justices are women. Could it be that my personal problems aren't just accidents because I have been very anti-feminist movement? I don't have statistics, insider information, or proof but there is one thing for certain that man should not ignore….THEY ARE EVERYWHERE!

The Sick and the Afflicted

It's a kind and Christian thing to do to pray for the sick and the afflicted. Over the years as our large family have suffered all the flues and colds common to mankind it has been interesting to note how each member handles illness. My first born, who is a daughter, a kind and gentle soul, likes to camp. She even got a job with a troubled youth wilderness survival group. Every other week throughout the winter she slept in the open in the snow and built her own fires and cooked her own meals over a camp fire. Self-defense training both on the job and extra-curricula have come in handy in handling the rougher elements of our society. She is not very big but she can take care of herself. You'd think that something like a little cold would be nothing for a tough little gal like that but no... when she is sick every body knows it. Mother climbs the stairs to her room twenty times a day for fear that the moaning and groaning means the illness has gotten critical but no, the little thing just needs comforting.

When my second born, a boy, on the other hand gets sick he goes to his room and climbs in bed and turns his face to the wall and when he is better he comes back down. He never makes a peep. He hates to be cold and as an adult he even moved to a warmer climate. Mom tries to remember to check on him but he is so quiet she tends to forget about him. I try to remind her to go doctor him but I forget too. Some of our other children have told us not to worry about it…if he dies, he in time will start to stink, then we can take care of it. His mother says that it is so convenient and easy to care for him he should get sick for everyone in the family.

My second son sits around and visits cheerfully with the family or goes to bed and lies quietly like his brother. Anyway we all have our personality traits.

I, on the other hand, enjoy the best traits of each. I'm tough like the first daughter but I suffer in silence alone in my room like the first son but when I am getting better I am cheerful and pleasant like the second son and like to spend time visiting with the family. I tell little jokes and make suggestions to the kids about their homework or how to do their chores more efficiently and little tips to the wife about house work. I lived alone for nine years when I was younger and I know a lot about that kind of stuff.

This last time when I got sick the whole family missed the convalescing part of my illness because I got an ear infection and temporarily lost my hearing and couldn't communicate. We were signing back and forth in an effort to communicate when the wife suddenly went and got a piece of paper and wrote me a note, "Dave, you don't have to sign to us. We can all hear! Talk to us." I felt a little silly but sitting in a silent world tends to color your thinking. It was a natural mistake...The next note said, "You don't have to yell - we can hear just fine!"

Word got around, I guess, that I had been ill and some of the brethren from the church stopped by to see me and to make sure that all was well at my house, I mean other than my hearing loss. It was quite gratifying, once I was able to go back to church, to discover that the congregation had included my name while praying for the sick. It was less gratifying to learn that they had included my wife and family when they had prayed for the afflicted and they weren't even sick.

It's All in Your Head

  Years ago I said to the wife that I didn't want to get old and not be able to do the things I wanted to, but now after all these years I find I don't want to do them anyway. Anybody that wanted to dance until dawn has got to be either very young or doesn't have a job to go to the next day... or week. A week end isn't enough any more for me to recover from such idiocy. I built a big house so the kids would have plenty of space to have their friends over. We would rather the kids have their parties, sleep overs and other of a hundred activities at our house than sit home and wonder if they were behaving themselves. It worked. Lewis and Roger were the same age as our children and they spent many hours daily at our house. Their mother told them that if they ate at our house one more time they would have to start calling my wife Mom. That afternoon they showed up at the door and said, "Hi, Mom!"

  The boy from the next town to the south fell in love with our second daughter and started coming by on a regular basis. Two nephews needed the experience of farm work or so their father said, so they came to spend the summer with us. It wasn't unusual to feed fifteen people for lunch that summer. In fact it was almost daily.

"How do you feed them all?" I was asked more than once.

"I feed them just like I do the animals…by the ton," I'd answer.

It is a good thing I owned a farm. We still have lots of people come by whether it be our children for a day or two or long time friends from town or out of town. The wife still likes to party and she stays up late; sometimes until one in the morning. While she has plenty of energy for the parties she complains of not having enough to clean our big house any more. I tell her if she would go to bed at nine o'clock like I do she wouldn't run out of steam before noon the next day. As you may have guessed it is a waste of breath, house cleaning can't compete with partying. Recognizing the truth of the matter I have come up with a solution. I have a nice spot out back where I could build a cozy little house with all the conveniences of modern day life. The children could buy the big house and the festivities could all take place there and when nine o'clock rolled around I could go home where it would be peaceful and quiet and I would get a good nights sleep and the wife could keep the place clean, not to mention the fact she could stay up as late as she wanted and then just walk away from the after party mess and come home.

Needless to say nobody but me likes this plan. The family all say I can just lay on my good ear and I won't hear a thing. While this may be true for a while, I might roll over in my sleep and get quite a shock. I've been known to say in the past that it is a good life if you don't weaken but now I've changed that to 'It's a good life if you don't waken.' Years ago I thought the epitome of happiness was a kiss from the girl friend. Later it was a night alone with the wife but in the last years nothing can compete with a good nights sleep.

While listening to me complain about being a slave to a big house that we don't need … you know with all the repairs and everything and with only two kids at home and the oldest threatening (I hope that's promising) to leave in three months … and with old age creeping upon me, the wife said,

"It's all in your head." She of course was referring to my old age.

I thought that over and decided that she is right…my hair and teeth are falling out, my eyes are getting dim and I have to wear a hearing aid. It's all in my head!

D.L. Hatton

CPSIA information can be obtained at www.ICGtesting.com
Printed in the USA
BVOW08s1321261213

340113BV00003B/432/P